PLAIN LANGUAGE LAW
Criminal Judicial Process
(Criminal Procedure)

by Garn H. Webb, Esq., B.S., LL.B.

Professional Impressions, Inc.
Publishers
Atlanta

PLAIN LANGUAGE LAW
Criminal Judicial Process (Criminal Procedure)

by Garn H. Webb, Esq.

Published by: Professional Impressions, Inc.
Corporate Offices:
203A - 180 Allen Road
Atlanta, Ga. 30328, U.S.A.

More books in the Plain Language Law series:

Corporations, 3rd Ed., 1981
Civil Wrongs (Torts), 3rd Ed., 1981
Criminal Wrongs (Crimes), 2nd Ed., 1981
Agency and Partnership, 3rd Ed., 1981
Civil Judicial Process (Civil Procedure), 3rd Ed., 1981

Copyright® 1981 by Professional Impressions, Inc.
First Edition 1979
Second Edition 1981
Printed and bound in United States of America

Library of Congress Cataloging in Publication Data.
Webb, Garn H., 1936-

Plain Language Law
Criminal Judicial Process (Criminal Procedure)
Bibliography: p. Includes index
I. Law II. Title III. Series
81-80339

ISBN 0-934098-14-X Series
ISBN 0-934098-17-4 Paperback
ISBN 0-934098-78-6 Hardcover

PLAIN LANGUAGE LAW
Criminal Judicial Process (Criminal Procedure)

Garn H. Webb, Esq., B.S., LL.B.

Editor
Forrest Wallace Cato, B.A., M.B.A.

Managing Editor
Christina S. Woodside, B.A.

Associate Editors

E. Lane Brown, B.A., LL.B.
R.E. Hodges, Jr., B.A., J.D.
Corporations • Agency and Partnership

John W. Knapp, Jr., Esq., B.A. LL.B.
Gary T. Lancaster, B.A.
Crimes • Criminal Procedure

Thomas M. Boyle, III, Esq., B.S., J.D.
Donald R. Minnich, B.S., M.B.A., Ph.D.
Civil Wrongs • Civil Procedure

This publication is designed to provide accurate and authoritative information in regard to the subject matter covered. It is sold with the understanding that the publisher is not engaged in rendering legal, accounting,
or other professional service. If legal advice or other expert assistance is
required, the service of a competent professional person should be sough

— From a Declaration of Principle
jointly adopted by a Committee
the American Bar Association and
Committee of Publishers and Assoc
ations.

CRIMINAL PROCEDURE

PART ONE: CRIMINAL PROSECUTION

I. *JURISDICTION*

III. *STATUTE OF LIMITATIONS*

IV. *DOUBLE JEOPARDY*

PART TWO: PRETRIAL PROCEEDINGS

I. *LEGAL PROCEEDINGS BEFORE TRIAL*

PART THREE: RIGHTS OF THE ACCUSED

I. *CONSTITUTIONAL PROTECTIONS*

II. *AFTER CONVICTION*

CRIMINAL PROCEDURE

PART ONE: CRIMINAL PROSECUTION

I. *JURISDICTION*

§1. OVER THE CRIME (THE SUBJECT MATTER)

A. AUTHORITY AND POWER OF THE COURT

1. *Power To Hear And Decide Criminal Case* —Before a trial court can render a valid judgment and sentence in a criminal prosecution, it must have jurisduction over **both** the *subject matter* (the crime) and the *person* (the accused). "Jurisdiction" is the **power** of a court to inquire into the facts of a case, to apply the law, and to declare the punishment. In other words, jurisdiction is the power to *hear* and *determine* a criminal prosecution. It encompasses every type of judicial action regarding the subject matter (the crime), from finding the indictment to pronouncing the sentence. (**Note:** The nationality or citizenship of the accused is **not** material to the issue of jurisdiction.)

   a. *Objection to jurisdiction over "subject matter" never waived* —The right of the accused to object to the court's lack of jurisdiction over the subject matter is *never waived* and may be raised at any stage of the proceedings. In other words, a conviction by a court that does not have jurisdiction over the crime is *invalid*. For example, if a statute requires that a particular crime must be tried by a jury, but the person accused of such crime is tried by a judge without a jury, he may, at any time, successfully object to the judge's lack of jurisdiction over the crime, even after the judge pronounces judgment.

1

2. *Crime Must Be Committed Within State* — A person is subject to criminal prosecution in the state where he is physically present whenever he commits a crime under the laws of that state. Jurisdiction in criminal proceedings rests **solely** in the courts of the state or country in which the crime is *committed* and the laws of each state or country *exclusively* govern the nature of the crime.

In order for a court to have jurisdiction over the crime, it must be committed wholly or partly **within** the state. That is, there must have been some *conduct* occurring in the state which is an element of the particular crime, or some *prohibited result* occurring within the state which is an element of the particular crime. For example, in larceny the "conduct" of the wrongdoer is an essential element of the crime and consists of the taking and carrying away of another's personal property by the accused or by someone for whom he is legally responsible; in murder the "result" of death is an essential element of the crime and consists of either physical contact which causes death (e.g., result of a bullet) or the death itself (e.g., result of arson).

a. *Concurrent jurisdiction within state* — The general rule is that the jurisdiction of a crime is in the **county** where the crime was committed. However, statutes in most states confer *concurrent* jurisdiction upon the courts of *each* county or district in which a crime was "in part" or "continuously" committed. When one of these courts takes active jurisdiction, the concurring jurisdiction of the other counties ceases. [**Note:** A "continuing" crime is a continuous unlawful act (kidnapping, false imprisonment) or a series of unlawful acts (multiple robberies).]

§2. OVER THE ACCUSED (THE PERSON)

A. PRESENCE WITHIN STATE

1. *Actual Presence (Conduct Within State)* — The *actual* or *constructive* presence of the accused within a state is considered essential to make his criminal act one which is committed within that state. Actual presence of the ac-

2

cused means his *physical* presence within the state. Thus, if the accused is within the state and commits a criminal act, the conduct or result of which also occurs within the state, the state has jurisdiction over the crime **and** over the accused.

2. *Constructive Presence (Result Within State)* —Acts performed outside a state, but which produce a prohibited result within it, will give the state jurisdiction over the crime and also over the person if he comes within the state. If a person in one state sets in motion a force which causes a prohibited "result" in another state, the actual presence of such person in the other state is *not* necessary in order to give it jurisdiction over the subject matter; however, the accused's presence *is* necessary to obtain jurisdiction over his person.

In the absence of statute, the courts of the state where the person accused was standing at the time he set the force in motion have *no jurisdiction* over the crime or the accused **unless** (1) the act is a crime in that state, or (2) it is a homicide case where the act was commmitted in one state and the death resulted in another. When there is conduct **within** the jurisdiction of a state which amounts to an attempt, solicitation, or conspiracy to commit a crime *outside* its borders (e.g., in another state), which is a crime under the laws of *both* states (e.g., both states have juridiction over the subject matter), then **either** state may take jurisdiction if the accused can be found within their respective state.

a. *Objection to jurisdiction over "person" may be waived*—Jurisdiction of the person of the accused may be acquired by consent of the accused or by his waiver of any objection *before* trial. If the accused fails to make his objection before trial, or pleads not guilty and goes to trial, he will be deemed to have waived his objection.

II. *VENUE*

§1. PLACE WHERE PROSECUTION BEGINS

A. LOCALITY OF CRIME

1. *County Where Crime Committed* — The term "venue", as applied to criminal cases, means the *place* where prosecutions are to *begin*. It describes the particular **county** (or territory) within a state or district in which the accused is to be brought to trial. The rule in all jurisdictions is that the proper venue of a crime is the county (or territory) where the crime was **committed**. Modern statutes generally provide that where a crime is committed partly in one county and partly in another, venue is in *either* county. In other words, the location of the person committing the crime may not necessarily be the county where the crime was committed.

   The general rule is that the crime is committed in the county of the state where the crime is "consummated" (e.g., the elements of the particular crime are fulfilled). For example, when a forged instrument is mailed to another county, the county where the instrument was received is where the crime was consummated and is the place of venue for the crime of uttering a forged instrument, and not the county in which it was mailed. (**Note:** Under the common law, when a crime is partly committed in one county and partly in another, there can be no prosecution in either unless enough was done in one of the counties that it would constitute a complete crime in and of itself.)

   a. *Venue in federal courts* — Under the 6th Amendment to the U.S. Constitution the trial of criminal prosecutions are required to take place in the state or district where the crime was *committed*. Rules 18 and 20 through 22 of the Federal Rules of Criminal

Procedure authorize the transfer of criminal cases (crimes against the United States) from one jurisdictional district to another for trial (e.g., a "change of venue"), either with the consent of the accused or at his request. Whether or not a criminal case should be transferred is within the *discretion* of the trial court.

b. *Waiver of venue*—The right of an accused to be tried in the county where the crime was committed is a personal right which *may* be waived. Venue is waived by a failure of the accused to make an objection *before* or *during* the trial.

2. *Distinguished From Jurisdiction*—The term "jurisdiction" refers to the judicial *power* to hear and determine a criminal prosecution, whereas the term "venue" refers to the particular *county* within a state in which the prosecution is to be brought or tried. The jurisdiction over a crime *cannot* be waived; the venue of the crime *can* be waived.

§2. CHANGE OF VENUE

A. RIGHTS OF ACCUSED PREJUDICED

1. *Right To Fair And Impartial Trial*—It is a fundamental principle of law that every person charged with crime shall have a right to a fair and impartial trial. The purpose of a change of venue is to provide the accused with a disinterested, unprejudiced, and unbiased trial. For example, a state law which does not permit a change of venue violates the right to trial by an impartial jury. The law presumes that an accused can get a fair and impartial trial in the county in which the crime was committed. When the accused can show that he will be unable to obtain a fair trial, he is entitled to have the venue changed to another county.

In order to overcome the presumption of a fair trial, the burden is on the accused to show that there is sufficient local excitement or prejudice against him in the county where the crime was committed to prevent a fair and impartial trial. The determination of whether or not local prejudice will result in an impartial trial rests within the sound discretion of the trial court. The test is whether a prospective juror can set aside his impression or opinion and render a verdict based on the evidence. For example, where individual jurors, on the basis of unfavorable publicity, have formed an opinion as to the accused's guilt *before* the trial begins, it is a denial of a fair and impartial trial.

Where there is *excessive* pretrial publicity which is prejudicial to the accused, it may require a change of venue. The accused must prove that because of adverse pretrial publicity (e.g., newspaper, television, radio, etc.) there is such a feeling of prejudice and bias against him in the proper county of venue that his right to a fair and impartial trial is jeopardized. Merely complying with the statutory formalities regarding application for a change of venue does *not*, as a matter of right, entitle the accused to a change of venue; he must also satisfy the court that the publicity is recent, widespread, and highly damaging, and therefore justifies the requested change.

a.   *Bias or prejudice of judge*—The **majority** of jurisdictions have statutes which provide for a change of venue in criminal actions on the ground of the bias, prejudice, or other disqualification of the trial judge. In a **minority** of jurisdictions, the bias or prejudice of the judge is not such a disqualification as will give the accused a right to a change of venue. (**Note:** At common law a change of venue is never allowed on the basis of a personal objection to the trial judge because of his incompetency or prejudice, or for any other reason applicable to him *personally*.)

2.   *Removal of Case to New County*—Modern statutes generally permit a change of venue from the county in which a criminal action has been properly brought to another county *within the state* when such a change is necessary to avoid local prejudices which might be detrimental to the rights of the accused if the case is tried in the proper county of venue. Statutes in many states provide that a change of venue must be to the nearest or adjoining

7

county. However, in the absence of such a statute, the removal may be made to any county within the state where, in the judge's opinion, the accused can obtain a fair and impartial trial.

III. *STATUTE OF LIMITATIONS*

§1. TIME LIMITATION FOR COMMENCEMENT OF PROSECUTION

A. FROM TIME CRIME COMMITTED

1. *No Prosecution After Expiration of Time Period* — A statute of limitation (as it applies to criminal procedure) defines that period of time, *after* a crime is committed, within which the state **must** begin its prosecution against any alleged perpetrator of the crime. In other words, no prosecution can be commenced *unless* it is begun within the specified statutory period after the crime was committed. The general rule is that after the expiration of such period of time no prosecution may be brought against anyone. The crime of murder is an exception to the general rule; that is, murder has **no** statute of limitations.

   The general rule is that a statute of limitations begins to run from the time the crime is **committed** (or when the crime is completed) until the prosecution is **commenced**. It does *not* run from the date the crime is discovered. Virtually every jurisdiction has enacted statutes of limitation which "limit" the time for commencement of most criminal proceedings. (**Note:** Under most statutes the day the crime was committed is *excluded* from the computation of time.) When the crime is "continuous" in nature, the statute begins to run from the occurrence of the most *recent* act and not from the occurrence of the initial act, even though such initial act may in itself embody all the elements of the crime.

   Depending on the rules of the particular jurisdiction, a prosecution is deemed to be commenced either (1) at the time when a formal written complaint or affidavit is filed in a preliminary proceeding, or (2) when a warrant which has been issued persuant to such complaint or affidavit is placed in the hands of an officer of the court for service.

As a general rule, most states have statutes of limitations which apply to all (or most) misdemeanors and those felonies not punishable by death (e.g., a crime not punishable by death may be required by statute to be prosecuted within two years after it is committed).

a. *No time limitation unless specified by statute*—If there is no statute of limitation for a particular crime, the prosecution may be commenced at any time *after* commission of the criminal act. That is, unless a period of limitation is fixed by statute for a particular crime, a prosecution for the crime is *not* barred by lapse of time.

IV. *DOUBLE JEOPARDY*

§1. SECOND PROSECUTION FOR SAME CRIME PROHIBITED

A. POTENTIAL RISK OF SECOND PUNISHMENT

1. *Second Punishment Forbidden By 5th and 14th Amendments*—One of the basic principles of the common law is that a person shall not be placed in danger of his life or limb more than once for a crime he is charged with committing. Under the 5th Amendment to the U.S. Constitution (and under most state constitutions) no person shall be twice put in jeopardy for the same crime. The 5th Amendment right to be free of double jeopardy has been "incorporated" into the 14th Amendment and made applicable to state actions.

The term "jeopardy", in a criminal prosecution, refers to the **"danger" of punishment** which an accused incurs when brought to trial before a court of competent jurisdiction. (**Note:** "Procedural" matters *preliminary* to a trial do **not** constitute jeopardy.)

The term "double jeopardy" refers to the **"danger"** of a **second punishment** which an accused incurs when brought to trial again for the *same* crime (or a lesser included crime). The double jeopardy rule **prohibits** a second prosecution for the same criminal act upon which a first prosecution was based. In other words, an accused *cannot* be retried for the same crime (or a lesser included crime).

Under the double jeopardy rule, a verdict of acquittal or conviction is a **bar** to a subsequent prosecution for the same crime. The double jeopardy rule not only prohibits a second punishment for the same crime, it also forbids a second prosecution or trial for the same crime. However, if the accused fails to raise the defense of former (previous) jeopardy at the commencement of a second prosecution, the protection against double jeopardy is *waived*.

11

The fact that a person has once been put in jeopardy for a particular crime is not a bar to a prosecution for a later *separate and distinct* crime. If a new fact develops after the first prosecution of the accused, and the new fact plus the previously existing facts constitute a *separate* crime, a conviction or acquittal in the first proceeding is *not* a bar to a prosecution for the new crime. For example, a conviction on a charge of battery will not bar a subsequent prosecution for murder if the victim later dies as a result of his injuries.

2. *Prosecution for Lesser "Included" Crime Constitutes Jeopardy* — In the **majority** of states (and in federal courts) a conviction or acquittal of a lesser crime which is a necessary part of the greater crime charged is an implied *acquittal* of the more serious crime. In other words, an acquittal or conviction of a lesser included crime will *bar* a subsequent prosecution for the greater crime. For example, an acquittal or conviction for larceny will bar a subsequent prosecution for robbery based on the same facts. Conversely, an acquittal or conviction for the more serious crime will bar a subsequent prosecution for a lesser "included" crime. For example, if an accused is acquitted of the charge of murder, it will bar a subsequent prosecution for manslaughter.

If a conviction of the lesser included crime is set aside on appeal, the accused may be retried only for the lesser included crime since he has been impliedly acquitted of the greater crime. For example, if a person is charged with murder, but is convicted of manslaughter, he may be retried only for manslaughter.

3. *When Different Crimes Committed At Same Time* — Under the double jeopardy rule, a single **crime** *may* constitute two or more separate and distinct crimes for which two or more separate punishments may be imposed. If there was one criminal act and intent, and the accused was prosecuted and convicted (or acquitted) of a crime based on such act and intent, no subsequent prosecution may be based thereon.

A single **act** *may* constitute two or more separate and distinct crimes (e.g., one shot from a gun injures or kills several persons) and, unless prohibited by statute, separate punishments may be imposed. As a practical matter, most jurisdictions permit multiple crimes resulting from one act to be *joined* and prosecuted in one trial so that there will be only *one* punishment imposed for all the crimes committed. A subsequent attempt to prosecute any of the crimes in a separate trial is prohibited under the Constitutional provision against double jeopardy.

A single **criminal transaction** *may* constitute two or more distinct and separate crimes for which separate punishments may be imposed (e.g., a planned series of robberies). That is, two or more separate and distinct acts committed during the *same* criminal transaction may constitute two or more crimes (e.g., during a burglary, the accused ties up the dwelling's occupants and robs them). (**Note:** The general rule is that prosecutions for separate crimes based on the same criminal transaction do *not* constitute double jeopardy when there are distinct elements in one crime that are not included in the other.)

a. ***Prosecution for "continuing" crime or portion of crime***—The general rule is that there can be only **one** prosecution for a *continuing* crime or for any *part* of a single crime. In other words, a conviction or acquittal based on a portion of a single crime or on a continuing crime will bar a subsequent prosecution based on the entire crime or another part of the same crime. The test is whether the same evidence is required to prove them; that is, whether the evidence that warranted an acquittal or conviction on the first charge would warrant an acquittal or conviction on the second charge.

4. *When Same Crime Violates State And Federal Law*—The same criminal act may constitute a violation of both federal **and** state laws (e.g., kidnapping). The general rule is that a conviction or acquittal in a state jurisdiction will not prevent a subsequent prosecution in the federal jurisdiction, and vice versa. This is the so-called "dual sover-

eignty" concept. For example, a prosecution in federal court for robbing a federally insured state bank does not bar a subsequent state prosecution based on the same robbery. The dual sovereignty concept does *not* apply where the same criminal act violates both a state law and a municipal ordinance since the municipal government and the state government are in actuality the *same* sovereignty.

B. WHEN JEOPARDY ATTACHES

1. *At Time Jury Or First Witness Sworn*—"Jeopardy" attaches when an accused is put on trial before a court of competent jurisdiction and the entire jury is **sworn** or, if there is no jury ("bench" trial with judge only), when the first witness has been **sworn**. Jeopardy also attaches when there is a plea of guilty under oath. (**Note:** "Double jeopardy" attaches when the second prosecution commences.)

Once a legally impaneled jury or the first witness has been sworn (e.g., jeopardy has attached) any unauthorized dismissal of the case or discharge of the jury is equivalent to an acquittal and will bar a subsequent trial on the same charge. The power to dismiss the case after the jury or the first witness is sworn, or to discharge the jury after it is impaneled, may be exercised only where, in the discretion of the court, there is a manifest **necessity**. In the absence of necessity, the general rule is that a subsequent discharge of the jury or dismissal of the case is an *acquittal*.

Double jeopardy does *not* prohibit retrial of an accused after a "mistrial" because the retrial is considered to be merely a continuance of the same prosecution. Similarly, a nolle prosequi, a dismissal with the accused's consent, or a termination of the trial for any other "legally sufficient" reason, does *not* operate as an acquittal or prevent further prosecution of the crime. For example, an accused will *not* be deemed to have been placed in jeopardy if a prosecution is terminated because of illness of the judge or jury, because a fair trial is impossible, or because of a hung jury (e.g., the jury cannot agree on a verdict).

2. *Res Judicata and Collateral Estoppel*—When there is a second prosecution of an accused for the same crime, the doctrine of double jeopardy applies. When there is a separate prosecution of an accused for a *second* crime, the doctrine of double jeopardy cannot apply because there is no identity of crimes. However, the doctrine of *res judicata* and *collateral estoppel* may apply to prohibit prosecution of any "issue" or "question" which was actually and legally adjudicated in the prior prosecution. The double jeopardy provision of the 5th Amendment *includes* the doctinre of collateral estoppel and has been made fully applicable to state actions by virtue of the 14th Amendment.

The term "res judicata" means that where a fact or question has been distinctly put in issue and has been finally and legally determined by the decision or verdict of a court of competent jurisdiction, such fact or matter is deemed to be conclusive and **cannot** be later disputed between the same parties. When applied to a criminal matter, a plea of res judicata is, in effect, an *estoppel* against the state from again prosecuting a matter which has already been determined in a *collateral* (previous) prosecution. In other words, the judgment or verdict in the first prosecution operates (under the doctrine of res judicata) as an estoppel **only** as to those matters which were in issue and *actually litigated* in the first prosecution.

PART TWO: PRETRIAL PROCEEDINGS

I. *LEGAL PROCEEDINGS BEFORE TRIAL*

§1. GRAND JURY

A. ACCUSING PERSON OF CRIME

1. *Presentment or Indictment (Felonies Only)*—The 5th Amendment to the U.S. Constitution provides, in part, that no person accused of committing a capital crime (penalty of death) or otherwise infamous crime (penalty of imprisonment) can be held and required to answer such accusation *unless* he has been accused by a "presentment" or "indictment" of a **Grand Jury**. In other words, in federal courts a person can be legally accused of a felony only by a Grand Jury. A **majority** of state constitutions also require Grand Jury indictment before an accused can be formally charged with committing a felony. The Constitution does not require, nor does it prohibit, a state from adopting the use of a Grand Jury as part of its judicial system.

A Grand Jury is a jury of "inquiry" composed of between twelve and twenty-three persons (unless otherwise provided by statute) whose duty it is to receive complaints and accusations in criminal cases, hear the evidence presented by the state (but *not* that of the accused) and to make a "presentment" or "indictment" if they believe the accused should be charged with committing a felony. The general rule is that a Grand Jury *can* consider evidence which would be inadmissible at a trial of the accused. In other words, a presentment or indictment is *not* invalid merely because it is based on inadmissible evidence. Thus, a witness before a Grand Jury *cannot* refuse to answer questions put to him on the ground that such questions are based on inadmissible evidence.

17

A *written* formal accusation by a Grand Jury stating that there is reasonable cause to believe that a person named therein has commited one or more *felonious* acts or crimes must be presented to the court in which it is impaneled before a person will be deemed to be formally charged with committing a felony. When the accusation by the Grand Jury is based on information from its *own* knowledge or observation, the accusation is called a **presentment**; when the accusation by the Grand Jury is based on a request by a state or federal prosecuting officer, and the information underlying the accusation is supplied by *such officer*, the accusation is called a **Grand Jury indictment**.

a. *No right to counsel* — Grand Jury proceedings are secret and neither the accused nor witnesses called to testify before the Grand Jury have the right to have an attorney present. The rationale is that at this stage of the prosecution the accused has not yet been formally charged and is therefore not entitled to an attorney to represent him in such proceedings.

b. *Petit jury distinguished* — A jury of "inquiry" is called a *grand* jury because it is composed of a greater number of persons than the ordinary trial jury summoned and impaneled for the trial of a case. The ordinary "trial" jury consists of a lesser number of persons than a grand jury and is called a *petit* jury.

2. *Information Or Accusation (Grand Jury Not Required)* — In those states which recognize the Grand Jury process, a person cannot be prosecuted for a *felony* until the Grand Jury has made a presentment or an indictment to the court. *Misdemeanors* do **not** require a Grand Jury accusation. When a person is to be charged with committing a misdemeanor (or committing a felony when state constitutions do not provide for a Grand Jury), the proper method of presenting such charges to the court is by an **information** or an **accusation** rather than by a presentment or an indictment. The "information" or "accusation" is a written formal charge which is placed before the court by the prosecuting officer for the state, *without* the intervention or approval of the Grand Jury.

18

§2. ARREST

A. MUST BE WITH PROBABLE CAUSE

1. *Detention of a Person*—A person is under arrest when a police officer has *restrained* him and the person is aware of that restraint. It is a detention of the person for purposes of subjecting him to criminal prosecution. An arrest is reasonable only if there was **"probable cause"** to believe that a crime has been or is being committed. No warrant is required where probable cause exists, even if there is an opportunity to obtain one. Probable cause to arrest requires only "reasonable belief". (**Note:** The term "police" usually refers to town or *city* officers. The term "sheriff" usually refers to a *county* officer. The term "highway patrol" usually refers to *state* police officers.)

   An arrest may be accomplished by either of the following: (1) **with a warrant** issued by a judge who has received evidence that the person named in the warrant has committed the crime; or (2) **without a warrant** when a police officer has probable cause to believe that a person *has* committed a felony or *is* committing either a felony or a misdemeanor, **and** unless immediately arrested, the person may cause injury to others, destroy evidence, or escape. When there is no Grand Jury indictment, the arrest warrant must be based on a formal charge made by a complaint or affidavit. If the arrest is made without a warrant, a complaint must be filed before further proceedings may be taken.

   [**Note:** In many states a person who is the victim of an *illegal* arrest is permitted to sue the policeman (or other person) who made the arrest for civil damages. The test, however, is whether the policeman acted reasonably under the circumstances, not whether the person arrested was actually guilty of the crime.]

2. *Police Station Detention*—A police station detention is not an arrest, it is merely an authorized detention of a suspect. The suspect is taken to the police station for purposes of conducting an investigation, with the intent of arrest only if further facts support the suspect's guilt.

19

In order for a police station detention to be valid, there must be (1) some objective basis for suspecting the person, (2) a reliable investigatory procedure such as fingerprinting, (3) the trip to the police station cannot be inconvenient to the suspect, and (4) a *court order* finding that there is adequate evidence to justify the detention. (**Note:** An **arrested** person may be fingerprinted, measured, and photographed *without* a court order. Such action is not an invasion of privacy nor is it a violation of the privilege against self-incrimination.)

§3. INITIAL APPEARANCE (PRETRIAL RELEASE OR DETENTION)

A. CHARGING PERSON WITH CRIME

1. *Must Be Brought Promptly Before Judge (Magistrate)* — An accused is deemed to be *formally charged* when a complaint or affidavit (presentment, indictment, information, or accusation) is presented to a court of competent jurisdiction. The complaint or affadavit may be presented to the court prior to arrest of the accused (e.g., issuing a warrant for his arrest); after arrest of the accused, but before the initial appearance (e.g., arrested while committing crime); or, at the initial appearance (e.g., arrested on suspicion of committing crime).

A person arrested with or without a warrant **must** be brought without unnecessary delay before a judge to be advised of his rights and the charges against him. By statute or court decision in all jurisdictions, an accused has a right to be **promptly** presented before a judge following arrest. This first confrontation between the accused and a "judicial" officer is referred to as the *initial appearance*. If the accused is to be charged with a state crime, the initial appearance will be before a judge in a state or local court; if the accused is to be charged with a federal crime, the initial appearance will be before a magistrate in the U.S. District Court.

At the initial appearance, the judge explains the accused's *constitutional rights*, informs him of the *charges* against him and his right to have a *preliminary hearing* (if a felony is charged), appoints a *lawyer* (if he does not already have one), and sets the next *court date*. If the crime charged is a misdemeanor, the initial appearance is frequently termed a "misdemeanor arraignment". [**Note:** An accused charged with committing a felony may enter his plea at the preliminary hearing or at the felony arraignment. An accused charged with committing a misdemeanor is *required* to enter his plea at the initial appearance (e.g., "guilty", "not guilty", or "nolo contendere").]

The judge must then determine whether or not to release the accused or keep him in custody. The judge will generally consider such factors as the accused's criminal record; the particular crime the accused is charged with committing, the accused's ties to the community (family, employment, school, etc.); and, whether (in the judge's opinion) the accused will appear for trial. He must then do one of the following:

(1) Release the accused until trial on his own word that he will appear in court at the time of trial (*personal recognizance*).

(2) Release the accused on condition that he pay a certain sum of money in order to insure that he will appear at the time of trial (*set bail or bond*). An accused is usually permitted to obtain a local bondsman to put up the bail. The money is ultimately returned to the accused or to the bondsman unless it is forfeited by the accused not appearing in court when required. If the accused cannot pay the money or the bondsman's fee, he will be held in jail until trial.

(3) Release the accused into the custody of another person, institution, or organization (*third–party custody*).

(4) Require that the accused to be held in custody without bail until trial whenever the judge believes the accused would be a threat or danger to the community if released (*preventive detention*). This usually occurs only when the accused is charged with a seri-

ous crime of violence or if he has previously been convicted of such a serious crime.

a. ***Right to counsel*** — The general rule is that the constitutional right to the assistance of counsel attaches when (1) the accused has been *formally charged* with the commission of a crime or (2) when it is necessary to meet the "fundamental fairness" test of due process. For example, a police *interrogation* of the accused after an indictment or an initial appearance violates the due process clauses of the 5th and 14th Amendments *unless* an attorney is present.

If a person is not formally charged with a crime between the time of his arrest and his initial appearance, he is *not* entitled to an attorney during such period. For example, an accused does not have the right to the presence of an attorney at a *lineup*, at a *showup* (confrontation between accused and a witness), or at a *photographic identification session* (a witness is shown photographs of suspects, including the accused), **unless** he has been formally charged with a crime.

§4. PRELIMINARY HEARING

A. JUDICIAL INQUIRY (NOT A TRIAL)

1. *Probable Cause Accused Committed Crime* — The general rule is that a preliminary hearing applies only to persons charged (accused) with committing a **felony** (capital or infamous crime). It is a pretrial examination of the charges against the accused in order to ascertain whether there is "probable cause" for the accusation against him; that is, whether there is sufficient evidence to warrant holding the accused (with or without bail) until his trial. It is not a trial to determine the accused's guilt or innocence; it is merely a judicial inquiry to determine whether there are reasonable grounds to believe a crime has been committed, and if so, whether there is probable cause to believe the accused committed the crime.

If a person has been accused of a crime by a Grand Jury

presentment or indictment *prior* to the preliminary hearing (before or after the initial appearance), the Grand Jury's action **preempts** the accused's right to a preliminary hearing. (**Note:** There is no fundamental right to a preliminary hearing under the U.S. Constitution and the denial of a preliminary hearing to a person charged with a felony does **not** violate the "due process" or "equal protection" clauses of the 5th or 14th Amendments.)

After a Grand Jury presents an indictment there is no right to a preliminary hearing since Grand Jury findings are also based upon probable cause. (**Note:** A preliminary hearing in federal courts applies only to a person who has been arrested for a felony *prior* to a Grand Jury indictment. Its purpose is to determine whether or not there is sufficient evidence against an accused to justify a Grand Jury proceeding.)

a. *Waiver of preliminary hearing* — Unless prohibited by statute, an accused may waive the right to a preliminary hearing by either voluntarily giving a bond or personal recognizance for his appearance in the trial court, pleading guilty to the crime charged, or pleading not guilty to a misdemeanor and going to trial. If the accused expressly *waives* his right to the preliminary hearing, or voluntarily *pleads guilty* to the crime charged, it is an "admission" by the accused that there is sufficient evidence to justify holding him for trial and the judge is not required to proceed further with the preliminary hearing.

In the absence of such waiver or plea the prosecuting officer need only present enough evidence to convince the judge that there is probable cause to believe that a crime was committed and that the accused committed the crime. If it appears to the judge that there is probable cause to believe the accused committed the crime (circumstantial evidence alone may be sufficient), the accused will be held for trial (bound over). If the judge finds no probable cause, the accused must be released.

§5. FELONY ARRAIGNMENT

A. OPPORTUNITY TO ENTER PLEA

1. *Required Where Felony Is Charged*—A felony arraignment is a separate court appearance *after* the initial appearance and preliminary hearing. The purpose of a felony arraignment is to identify the accused by naming him, to inform him of the charges against him by reading the indictment, to give him an opportunity to enter his plea to such charges, and to record his plea. If the plea is "guilty", the judge sets the date for trial; if the plea is "not guilty" or "nolo contendere", the judge sets the date for sentencing.

   In the **majority** of jurisdictions, an arraignment is required for *felony* cases; that is, it is *necessary* to a valid felony conviction unless waived by the accused. (**Note:** It is a fundamental right of the accused to be informed of the charges against him and to be given an opportunity to plead; except where modified by statute, a conviction for a felony must be reversed if there was no felony arraignment of the accused.)

   a. *Waiver*—The right to an arraignment may ordinarily be waived, provided the accused knows the nature of the charge against him and has a full opportunity to defend himself. The accused may waive the arraignment by voluntarily entering a plea of guilty, by expressly waiving it in open court, by announcing ready for trial, or by going to trial without objection.

2. *Plea Bargaining*—A "plea bargain" is a negotiation between the attorney for the accused and the prosecuting officer whereby, in exchange for a guilty plea or for information concerning the crime, the prosecutor agrees to permit the accused to either plead guilty to a *lesser included* crime than is charged or to grant him *immunity*. For example, if the charge is robbery, the prosecutor may agree to reduce the charge to larceny (which carries a lesser penalty) in exchange for a plea of guilty. The prosecutor can make a "bargain" only with respect to the **charges** against the accused. The prosecutor *cannot* make a bargain with respect to the *sentence* imposed; sen-

tencing is within the exclusive jurisdiction of the judge. (**Note:** A plea bargain agreement is not binding on the court; that is, the judge is *not* required to accept the agreement and may require a plea to the original charge.)

Before the judge accepts a *guilty* plea, he must determine that the accused understands he is waiving certain fundamental rights (the right to trial, the right to proof beyond a reasonable doubt, the right to cross-examine witnesses, etc.). It is not necessary that the accused openly admit that he actually committed the acts charged; he need only plead guilty to the charges. (**Note:** The general rule is that when an accused pleads guilty pursuant to a plea bargain, he will be permitted to withdraw his guilty plea if the prosecution does not keep the bargain.)

B. PLEAS OF ACCUSED

1. *Plea of Not Guilty*—Under due process of law the accused has an absolute right to an opportunity to plead, and the fact that such opportunity was furnished *must* appear affirmatively in the record before his trial can legally proceed. The plea of not guilty **creates the issue** for trial. In other words, there can be no trial on the merits in a criminal case unless the accused has previously pleaded *not guilty*. The general rule is that if the accused remains silent or refuses to plea, it is equivalent to a not guilty plea and the judge must enter a plea of not guilty and proceed to trial.

2. *Plea of Guilty*—By a plea of guilty, the accused **waives** the right to trial and the Constitutional guarantees with respect thereto. The general rule in both state and federal courts is that the judge cannot accept a plea of guilty without first determining that the plea is made intelligently and voluntarily by an accused who is competent to understand the consequences of such a plea. That is, the record **must** show that the accused was aware of his rights at trial and *knowingly* and *voluntarily* waived them. These rights include the right to a jury trial, the right to confront witnesses, the right to attack the legality of a search and seizure, the right to be protected against self-incrimination, and the right to have guilt proved beyond a

25

reasonable doubt. (**Note:** It is a denial of due process of law to induce a guilty plea by coercion, deception, trick, threat, or other such inducement.)

a. *Equivalent to a conviction*—An accused, by pleading guilty, waives all defenses; it is an admission of all the material facts necessary to convict and is as conclusive as the verdict of a jury. In other words, there is no distinction between the *effect* of a voluntary plea of guilty and a conviction at a trial on the merits. Upon its acceptance and entry by the court, a plea of guilty is the equivalent of a conviction.

b. *Withdrawal of plea*—The general rule is that an accused who has entered a plea of guilty is *not* entitled to *withdraw* such plea as a matter of right. It is within the sound discretion of the trial court as to whether a plea of guilty will be permitted to be withdrawn. In the **majority** of jurisdictions a plea of guilty may *not* be withdrawn after the accused has been convicted or sentenced. However, a conviction will be reversed if an abuse of discretion can be shown (e.g., denial of the constitutional right to counsel).

3. *Plea of Nolo Contendere*—A plea of "nolo contendere" is a formal declaration by the accused that he is unwilling to plead and present a defense, and that he does *not* wish to contest the charges against him. The **majority** of states do not recognize a plea of nolo contendere under any circumstances or have limited its application to misdemeanor charges only. The federal courts and a **minority** of states recognize the plea of nolo contendere in both felony and misdemeanor cases.

The plea of nolo contendere is *not* a matter of right with the accused. Acceptance of the plea is within the discretion of the court. Nolo contendere means "no contest". It raises no issue of law or fact and the court *cannot* hear testimony regarding the accused's guilt after having accepted the plea. The plea **cannot** be used against the accused in any subsequent civil suit for the same act, nor as an admission of guilt in any subsequent criminal prosecution. A conviction *after* a plea of nolo contendere has been accepted is a violation of the constitutional protection against double jeopardy and must be reversed.

a. *Distinguished from guilty plea* — The effect of a plea of nolo contendere, when accepted by the court, is equivalent to a plea of guilty, but is **limited** to the particular case. A plea of guilty is an admission of all charges and will bind the accused in further legal proceedings; the plea of nolo contendere is an admission of all charges, but has no effect beyond the particular proceeding.

b. *Withdrawal of plea* — Once a plea of nolo contendere has been accepted by the court, it may not be withdrawn as a matter of right. It is within the discretion of the court to permit the accused to withdraw the plea and replace it with another plea.

4. *Plea of Double Jeopardy* — The plea of double jeopardy is not a denial of any allegations of the indictment, nor does it constitute a plea of not guilty. It is a defense based on a collateral matter determined by a court on a previous occasion and is *not* a plea on the merits. If the accused can show that the second prosecution is based on the same criminal act (both in fact and in law) which was the basis of the first prosecution, he must be released and the case *dismissed*.

5. *Nolle Prosequi (No Prosecution)* — A "nolle prosequi" is an **unqualified dismissal** of an indictment by the prosecuting officer (attorney) which constitutes a *termination* of the prosecution against the accused. It is a formal entry into the court's record by the prosecuting officer whereby he declares that he is either unwilling to prosecute a case, or that he will not prosecute the case further. The court must immediately dismiss the case and release the accused. It is within the sole discretion of the *prosecuting officer* to enter a nolle prosequi (unless prohibited by statute). However, it must be entered *before* the jury is impaneled and sworn.

PART THREE: RIGHTS OF THE ACCUSED

I. *CONSTITUTIONAL PROTECTIONS*

§1. DUE PROCESS (FAIR AND IMPARTIAL PROCEEDINGS)

A. GUARANTEED BY 5TH AND 14TH AMENDMENTS

1. *Fundamental Fairness*—The 5th and 14th Amendments to the U.S. Constitution (and similar provisions in state constitutions) protect every person accused of crime by providing that *no citizen* shall be deprived of life, liberty, or property without "due process" of law. Due process requires that the accused be given reasonable *notice* of the charges against him and an adequate opportunity to be *heard* and defend against them. In other words, every person charged with crime has an absolute and fundamental right to a fair and impartial trial, regardless of whether the crime charged is a felony or a misdemeanor. (**Note:** The prosecution, as well as the accused, is entitled to a fair trial.)

   Due Process requires that there be a trial in a court having jurisdiction of the case, before an impartial judge and jury, and under conditions where there is no bias or prejudice for or against the accused. For example, an accused may be denied a fair trial by the presence of a hostile crowd, the bias of the judge, denying the accused a fair and reasonable time to prepare his defense, or other such prejudicial circumstances. (**Note:** Due process does **not** require that a convicted defendant be given a right to *appeal* a criminal conviction. However, if the defendant claims that he was deprived of his constitutional rights, due process **does** require that the state provide some "corrective process" by which he can prove his claim and obtain a remedy.)

29

The due process clause imposes a legal duty upon judicial and law enforcement officers to protect the basic constitutional rights of an accused person. Failure to provide an accused with the right to examine adverse witnesses, the right to offer testimony, or the right to be represented by counsel, violates even minimal standards for a fair hearing required by due process. For example, if an accused is totally or partially blind, deaf, or mute, it is the duty of the court to adopt procedures which will guarantee that he is not denied a fair and impartial trial because of his disability.

a. *Impartial judge* — Due process also requires that the judge be impartial and mentally competent. The accused has a right to have a judge who will remain impartial throughout the entire proceedings. If the judge is biased either for or against the accused, he must disqualify himself. If a judge will not disqualify himself, it is grounds for an appeal. For example, a criminal trial before a judge who is related to the accused or a judge who has a direct substantial pecuniary interest in convicting the accused is a denial of due process. (**Note:** A judge is *not* impartial or biased merely because he develops a particular dislike for the accused.)

b. *Prosecutor's duty to disclose material evidence* — Due process also requires that, upon request of the accused, the prosecutor must turn over all evidence in his possession which is **material** to the accused's defense. There is no right to evidence in possession of the prosecution which is not material to the case. Suppression or withholding of such evidence from the accused is a denial of due process, regardless of the good or bad faith of the prosecutor. [**Note:** The accused (or his attorney) has a right to interview witnesses and other persons who have knowledge of matters bearing on the crime. However, there is no right to interview a witness in jail (or a public institution); it is a privilege which may or may not be granted in the sound discretion of the court.]

Nondisclosure of material evidence denies due process even if it is merely negligent. For example, a failure by the prosecutor to inform the defense attorney that there was a promise of immunity in return for the accused's testimony is "material"; nondisclosure of such promise violates the accused's right to an opportunity to defend. It is also a denial of the accused's right to due process if the prosecutor knowingly uses perjured testimony or fails to correct the testimony of a witness which he knows to be false.

2. *Presumption of Innocence* —Due process requires that in all criminal cases the guilt of the accused must be proven *beyond a reasonable doubt* (civil cases require a preponderance of the evidence). A person accused of crime is **presumed to be innocent** until he is proven guilty "beyond" a reasonable doubt. In the absence of such proof he is entitled to an acquittal. It is a presumption (or inference) of law which places the burden of proof upon the state. In other words, the presumption of innocence is *not* evidence, it merely determines the burden of proof.

Since crimes are usually committed in secret and under conditions where concealment is highly probable, the guilt of one accused of a crime may be proved by *circumstantial evidence*. In order for circumstantial evidence to be admissible, the circumstances must all concur to show that such person committed the crime, it must create a presumption of guilt, and it must rebut the presumption of innocence.

Evidence that the accused committed *other crimes* at other times (even though of the same nature as the crime charged) is inadmissible and must be excluded unless there is some legal connection between the two; that is, where one tends to establish the other or some essential fact in issue. (**Note:** As a general rule evidence of other criminal acts is admissible to prove the accused's identity, knowledge, intent, motive, a common criminal scheme or plan, and, that the crime was not committed as a result of inadvertence, accident, or mistake.)

B. RIGHT TO BE PRESENT

1. *At All Stages of Trial*—The right of an accused to be present at all stages of his own trial is protected in federal courts by the due process clause of the 5th Amendment. The presence of the accused in state courts is required under the due process clause of the 14th Amendment *only* to the extent that an accused would be denied a fair and impartial trial if he were absent. For example, a trial of the accused which is held without his knowledge or which has improperly excluded him from being present is a denial of due process under the 5th and 14th Amendments (it is also a denial of the right to confront adverse witnesses under the 6th Amendment).

   The term "all stages of the trial" means that period of time *from* the beginning of the jury selection through the rendition of the verdict *to* the final discharge of the jury. In the **majority** of states the right to be present at "all" stages of the trial is limited to *felony* prosecutions. A **minority** of states provide that a person charged with committing a misdemeanor also has the right to be present at all stages of his trial.

   a. *When accused is " disruptive"*—An important part of the right to a fair and impartial trial is the right of an accused to make his appearance at trial free from all shackles, handcuffs, or other bonds. An accused who has been handcuffed or shackled without necessity will prejudicially influence a fair and impartial determination of guilt or innocence by the jury. However, the trial court does have discretion to have the accused handcuffed or shackled during the trial whenever there is an **immediate necessity** to do so in order to prevent violent conduct or escape by the accused. When an accused excessively disrupts the courtroom, the trial judge, in his discretion, may: (1) bind him and keep him in the courtroom; (2) hold him in contempt of court; or (3) remove him from the courtroom for the trial, but provide him with access to the trial (e.g., closed circuit T.V., a microphone, etc.).

b. ***Accused must be competent to stand trial*** — It is a violation of due process to put an accused on trial if he is not mentally present or fully conscious of what is going on (e.g., incompetent). Unless the accused's condition was voluntarily self-induced, he must be mentally, as well as physically, present; that is, he must be capable of understanding the charges and proceedings against him and co-operating with his lawyer in order to prepare his defense. The accused's right to be tried only while competent cannot be waived merely because he fails to assert it. That is, a trial court judge has a *continuing and independent* duty to be aware of evidence of the accused's incompetency, and, if such evidence appears, to stop the trial and make a determination of the accused's competency before proceeding further.

2. *At Rendition of Verdict* — The general rule is that when the charge is a felony, the accused has a right to be present at the rendition of the verdict. If the accused is in **custody** at the time the jury is to render its verdict, he *cannot* waive his right to be present, but must be brought into the courtroom. The right to be present at the verdict *can* be waived in misdemeanor cases.

a. ***"Polling" the jury*** – In the **majority** of jurisdictions, the accused has a right to have the jury "polled" after its verdict, provided he makes a timely request to do so. The polling of the jury is a procedure whereby each juror is required to state his individual verdict. The purpose of polling the jury is to determine that no juror has been coerced or induced to agree to the verdict and a unanimous verdict has, in fact, been agreed upon.

3. *At Sentencing* — An accused has a right to be present at the time sentence or judgment is pronounced against him, even in prosecutions for misdemeanors which are punishable merely by a fine. The right to be present at sentencing is *separate and apart* from the right to be present at the trial and rendition of the verdict. The general rule is

that a sentence passed in the absence of the accused is void; however, it does *not* void the verdict nor does it require a new trial.

§2. EQUAL PROTECTION (EQUAL AND IMPARTIAL JUSTICE)

A. GUARANTEED BY 14TH AMENDMENT

1. *All Persons and Classes of Persons* — By their terms, the first eight amendments to the U.S. Constitution apply only to encroachment by the *federal* government upon individual rights. However, the Supreme Court has safeguarded most of these amendments from encroachment of *state* governments by incorporating them into the 14th Amendment prohibitions against any **state** action which: (1) abridges (violates) the *privileges or immunities* of citizens of the U.S.; (2) deprives any person of life, liberty, or property without *due process of law*; or, (3) denies any person the *equal protection of the law*.

The following amendments to the U.S. Constitution guaranteeing individual rights relating to criminal procedure are now constitutionally protected by virtue of being "incorporated" by the Supreme Court under the equal and impartial protection of the 14th Amendment; (1) *4th Amendment* (protections): unreasonable searches conducted without a warrant, and exclusion of illegally obtained evidence; (2) *5th Amendment* (protections): self-incrimination, double jeopardy, Grand Jury indictment, and due process; (3) *6th Amendment* (rights): speedy trial, arraignment, public trial, trial by jury, confrontation of witnesses, compulsory process, and right to counsel; (4) *8th Amendment*: cruel and unusual punishment, and excessive bail or fines.

The term "equal protection" refers to equality between persons or classes of persons and **not** to equality or uniformity between territorial or geographic areas. Although the equal protection clause provides that no state can deprive a person of his right to equal and impartial justice under the law, the states are permitted a wide scope of discretion to enact criminal laws and procedures in order to deal with crime within their borders. (**Note:** Mere *laxity* in the enforcement of the criminal laws, however long continued, is *not* a denial of equal protection.)

The general rule is that a state *cannot* impose a penalty upon one person (or class of persons) for an act he (or they) commits and yet impose no penalty upon another person (or class of persons) for committing the same act. However, a person guilty of violating the criminal law is *not* entitled to protection under the equal protection clause merely because others equally guilty have not yet been prosecuted. Also, an accused person is entitled to reasonable and equal protection by the state while in police *custody*. The state has the absolute right to hold prisoners for crimes against it; however, it also has an absolute duty to protect them from any assault or injury while being so held.

a. ***Appeal of conviction by indigent (destitute) defendants*** — The U.S. Constitution does *not* require a state to grant appellate review of a criminal conviction (e.g., there is no constitutional "right" to appeal a judgment or conviction). However, if a state does grant such review, it must *not* make it less accessible to the poor than to the rich; that is, it violates the equal protection clause if it discriminates against convicted defendants because of their poverty. In other words, destitute defendants must be accorded an adequate appellate review just as fully as that available to those who can afford to pay for it. (**Note:** Indigents must be provided with counsel at state expense when a first appeal is granted by the state to all persons as a matter of right.)

§3. UNREASONABLE SEARCH AND SEIZURE PROHIBITED

A. GUARANTEED BY 4TH AMENDMENT

1. *Right of People to be Secure* —The 4th Amendment to the U.S. Constitution provides: "The right of the people to be secure in their persons, houses, papers, and effects, against unreasonable searches and seizures, shall not be violated, and no Warrants shall issue, but upon probable cause, supported by Oath or affirmation, and particularly

describing the place to be searched, and the persons or things to be seized." The right to be free from unreasonable searches and seizures contained in the 4th Amendment has been "incorporated" into the *due process* clause of the 14th Amendment and is enforceable in state actions. Thus, each state is free to develop its own laws concerning arrests, searches, and seizures in order to meet the needs of its local law enforcement, **provided** such laws do not violate the 4th Amendment's prohibition against unreasonable searches and seizures.

a. *Search* — A "search" is any violation of a person's reasonable and justifiable expectation of privacy regarding his person, house, papers, and effects. For example, a careful exploration of the outer surfaces of a person's clothing all over his body in an attempt to find weapons is a "search".

b. *Seizure* — A "seizure" is any exercise of dominion or control of a thing. Similarly, any detention of a person is a seizure and therefore must be reasonable within the meaning of the 4th Amendment. For example, whenever a police officer accosts an individual and restrains his freedom to walk away, he has "seized" that person. Thus, a search ordinarily implies a *quest* by an officer of the law, whereas a seizure contemplates a *forcible dispossession* or *detention*.

The basic purpose of the 4th Amendment is to safeguard an individual's right to *privacy* and *security* against arbitrary intrusions by governmental officials. In other words, the 4th Amendment protects **people**, not places. The protection against unreasonable searches and seizures applies to every person whether a minor, an adult, on the streets, in the home, the innocent, and those suspected or known to be criminals. [**Note:** The 4th Amendment applies to *corporations*. However, corporations are not entitled to all constitutional protections which private individuals have against searches and seizures (e.g., the right to privacy, self-incrimination, etc.)]

Those things a person knowingly exposes to the public,

even in his own home or office, are *not* protected by the 4th Amendment; however, those things a person seeks to preserve as *private*, even in an area accessible to the public, are protected. For example, the contents of first-class mail, consisting of letters and sealed packages subject to letter postage, moving entirely within the country, are protected by the 4th Amendment. (**Note:** When in the custody of postal authorities, only first class mail is entitled to the protection of the 4th Amendment.)

2. *Search Must Be Reasonable* — The 4th Amendment requires that both the search *and* the seizure be **reasonable**. In each case the determination of the reasonableness of a search and seizure must be decided on its own facts and circumstances. The need of the government to search or seize is balanced against the invasion of privacy and security which the search or seizure entails.

The general rule is that a search and seizure is always unreasonable unless a judicial warrant authorizing such search and seizure has been previously obtained; that is, the authority to search and seize must be evidenced by a *warrant*. (**Note:** A warrant will not be issued unless there is sufficient *probable cause* to believe that a crime is about to be or has been committed.) The **only** exception to this rule is when the burden of obtaining a warrant would frustrate the governmental purpose behind the search and seizure (e.g., destruction of evidence, escape of suspect, preventing a crime, etc.).

a. *Exploratory search (unreasonable)* — A search must be one in which officers are looking for specific articles, and must be conducted in a manner reasonably calculated to uncover such articles; any search more extensive than this constitutes a general "exploratory" search and is an unreasonable search and seizure. The officer must confine his search strictly to what is minimally necessary and cannot conduct a general exploratory search for whatever evidence of criminal activity he might find. In other words, a general exploratory search conducted merely in the hope that some evidence of criminal activity will be revealed is unlawful.

37

B. PROBABLE CAUSE ALWAYS REQUIRED

1. *Crime Has Been or is Being Committed*—The 4th Amendment does not forbid all searches and seizures; it only forbids *unreasonable* searches and seizures. The officers conducting the search must have **probable cause** to believe that they will find the instrumentality of a crime or evidence pertaining to a crime where they intend to search. Probable cause exists where the facts and circumstances within the officer's knowledge, and of which he has reasonably trustworthy information, are sufficient in themselves to justify a man of reasonable caution (a prudent person) in believing that a crime has been or is being committed or that the person to be arrested has committed or is committing a crime. (**Note:** An officer may rely upon information received through an informant, rather than upon his direct observations, so long as the informant's statement is reasonably corroborated by other matters within the officer's knowledge.)

   Probable cause is a *minimum* requirement for a reasonable search permitted by the Constitution. Only the probability, not the certainty, of criminal activity is the standard of probable cause. It means more than a simple assertion by the police (e.g., suspicion); there must be a reasonable basis for a belief that a crime has been or is being committed. There must be probable cause that there is something to seize where the officer intends to search; that is, sufficient evidence to justify a reasonable person in believing that the items specified, if found, should be seized as material evidence. For example, a search for specific stolen or contraband goods, with or without a warrant, is reasonable only where there is probable cause to believe that they will be uncovered in a particular location.

2. *There Must Be Warrant Based On Probable Cause*—In order for a search to be reasonable under the 4th Amendment, it must be supported by *probable cause* **and** it must be made pursuant to a *judicial warrant*. That is, the police, if they have time, must obtain a search warrant from a judge. Facts known to police officers which would be

sufficient to justify the issuance of a search warrant will **not** justify a search by the officers without a warrant. The sufficiency of the facts to support the search warrant must be drawn by a neutral and detached judge and not by the police officers.

Before a search warrant can be issued, there must be a connection (nexus) between the search and seizure and the specific criminal activity complained of. The judicial officer issuing the warrant must be supplied with sufficient information to make an *independent* judgment that there is probable cause to believe evidence or instrumentalities of crime will be found in the place to be searched, which, when seized, will aid in either apprehension or conviction. For example, the unexplained possession of mere property, without more, does not raise the presumption that the property was stolen. There must also be *other evidence* which tends to show the accused's **participation** in the crime. However, the unexplained possession of recently *stolen* property *does* raise a rebuttable presumption of theft or guilty possession. Evidence that such "fruits" of the crime were found in the accused's possession shortly after the commission of the crime is admissible in evidence against him.

a. *Administrative inspections* — Administrative inspections (pursuant to fire, health, or housing codes) of a *personal* residence, where there is no emergency requiring immediate access, are "significant intrusions" upon 4th Amendment rights and constitute a search within the meaning of the 4th Amendment. In the absence of valid *consent*, an administrative inspection may be made **only** pursuant to a warrant. Inspections by a governmental official to determine whether *commercial* premises are in compliance with health and safety regulations (electical wiring requirements, etc.) are also within the 4th Amendment protection. (**Note:** Such rules do *not* apply to inspections under the *liquor* laws.)

There must be probable cause (reasonable grounds) to believe that a violation exists on the premises sought to be inspected before the warrant will issue. [**Note:** A showing of "reasonable legislative or administrative standards" (e.g., the passage of time since the last inspection, conditions of the area in which the premises are located, etc.) is *not* sufficient probable cause for the issuance of the search warrant.

When an administrative agency **subpoenas** corporate books or records, the subpoena must be sufficiently limited in scope, relevant in purpose, and specific in its direction. For example, a search through all the records of a private corporation, relevant or irrelevant, in the hope that something tending to incriminate the corporation may turn up, exceeds the investigatory power of the agency and violates the 4th Amendment.

3. *Persons, Houses, Papers, and Effects Protected*—The 4th Amendment protects against searches and seizures of the **person**. For example, an individual in a business office, in a friend's apartment, or in a taxi cab, may rely upon the protection of the 4th Amendment. Similarly, the acts of government agents in attaching a listening device to a telephone booth and recording the occupant's end of the conversation constitutes an unreasonable search and seizure within the meaning of the 4th Amendment. (**Note:** A "seizure" of a person occurs only where the officer, by means of physical force or show of authority in some way, *restrains the liberty* of the person.)

The extracting of matter from the stomach or from the mouth (in order to prevent it from being swallowed), rectal and vaginal probes, and the *compulsory* administration of a blood test, constitute searches of "persons" under the 4th Amendment. The 4th Amendment prohibits any intrusions into a person's body on the mere chance that the desired evidence may be obtained. Searches into "body cavities" are reasonable *only* when there is probable cause and when conducted in a medically approved manner in hygenic surroundings.

The extraction of blood samples for testing is reasonable without a warrant only where it is done by a physician in a hospital environment according to accepted medical practices. For example, a blood sample to determine the alcohol content of blood may be taken from a person arrested for driving while intoxicated, provided it is done in a reasonable and medically approved manner.

A search of a *house* (residential premises) or private commercial premises including a business office, is presumed to be unreasonable unless it has been authorized by a valid search warrant. Mere belief that an article sought is concealed in a dwelling does **not** justify the search of such dwelling without a warrant.

The word "houses" used in the 4th Amendment has been enlarged by the courts to include the grounds and buildings immediately surrounding a dwelling. (**Note:** Objects seized on the lawn or grounds around a house are ordinarily not protected by the constitutional provision against unreasonable searches and seizures, unless the grounds are surrounded by a *fence*.) Also, a *temporarily unoccupied* dwelling falls within the constitutional protection against unreasonable search and seizure. For example, a room which has been rented in a hotel, motel, or rooming house is protected by the 4th Amendment, even if the search was consented to, or participated in, by a night clerk, the landlord, or the hotel or motel manager. (**Note:** The 4th Amendment's protection also extends to the renter of a public locker at public terminals.)

The congregation of a large number of persons in a private home does not transform it into a public place open to the police. However, when the home is converted into a commercial center to which outsiders are invited for purposes of transacting "unlawful" business, it is *not* protected by the 4th Amendment. Similarly, the mere fact that "suspects" are in an automobile is not enough to justify a search of the automobile without a warrant. If an arrest for a traffic violation is a mere pretext for a general exploratory search, the search will not be sustained. In other words, probable cause to arrest a person for a traffic violation is *not* sufficient probable cause for a warrantless search of his car for contraband or weapons.

Papers and effects which are subject to search warrants

include documents, books, papers, any other tangible objects, and oral statements. The *compulsory* production of
private papers, whether under a search warrant or a subpoena may constitute an unreasonable search and seizure
if they are to be used against the person or his property in
a criminal proceeding (e.g., seizure and sale of property
for the collection of federal taxes). When the object of a
search and seizure of private papers is to compel a person
to be a witness against himself in violation of the 5th
Amendment, it is an unreasonable search and seizure
within the 4th Amendment.

C. THE WARRANT

1. *Authority For Search And Seizure* — An application for a
   search warrant is a request for permission to search particular premises; it insinuates an existing violation of law
   and impliedly represents that there is a necessity to
   search. The purpose of a search warrant is to *authorize*
   the officer to conduct the search, and to *describe* the
   premises to be searched and the items for which the officer is authorized to search.

   Under federal rules, a warrant may be issued to search
   for and seize any (1) property that constitutes evidence of
   the commission of a crime; or (2) contraband, the fruits of
   crime, or things otherwise criminally possessed; or (3)
   property designed or intended for use, or which has been
   used, as the means of committing a crime. Most states
   have similar provisions. In other words, a warrant may be
   issued to search for and seize any property that constitutes "evidence" that a crime is being, or has been, committed. (**Note:** There is no common law right to issue
   search warrants.)

2. *Affidavits of Probable Cause* — The initial application for
   a search warrant is generally by an *affidavit* of probable
   cause. The primary function of an affidavit is to set forth
   the facts upon which the judge issuing the warrant may
   base his determination of whether sufficient probable
   cause exists for making the desired search or seizure. In
   some jurisdictions the affidavit is the sole basis for the
   determination of probable cause; in other jurisdictions the

judge may be permitted or required to take testimony under oath in addition to the affidavit.

A search warrant must be issued upon a *sworn* affidavit establishing the grounds for its issuance. The affidavit must set forth the facts showing the existence of *probable cause*. It need not be determined whether the specific crime charged has actually been committed; the only concern is whether there are reasonable grounds, at the time of the making of the affidavit and the issuing of the warrant, for believing that a crime has been, or is being, committed on the particular premises to be searched. Where the affidavit does not provide a sufficient basis for a finding of probable cause, and a search warrant issues, the evidence obtained as a result of such a search warrant is *inadmissible* in a criminal trial. There must be probable cause that there is something to seize where the officer intends to search; that is, sufficient evidence to justify a reasonable person in believing that the items specified, if found, should be seized as material evidence.

a. ***Informers*** — Hearsay evidence (not within personal knowledge) may be properly included in a supporting affidavit for a search warrant provided there is a reliable basis for such information. For example, police officers engaged in a common investigation are a reliable basis for an affidavit by one of their number. An affidavit *cannot* establish probable cause for the issuance of a search warrant if it merely states *suspicion or belief*, without stating the facts and circumstances upon which that belief is based.

Where the affidavit is based on information supplied by an *informant*, it must contain enough specific facts to permit the judge to determine for himself that the informant is a *generally reliable person*, and that the informant obtained his information in a manner that justifies relying on it (e.g., presence, personal observation, etc.). The reliability factor is satisfied when: (1) the informant is a person of a generally reliable group such as a police officer or a victim of a crime; (2) the officer has determined the informer's reliability by questioning him; or (3) the informant has, by giving the information, incriminated himself. In addition to the requirement of reliability the affidavit must include some factual information independently *corroborative* of the hearsay information. (**Note:** The general rule is that the identity of the informer need **not** be disclosed.)

3. *Description of Place, Person, or Thing* — The 4th Amendment provides that a search warrant must **particularly describe** the place to be searched and the persons or things to be seized; it prohibits general warrants. The description of a *place* is sufficient if the officer with the warrant can, with reasonable effort, ascertain and identify the place intended. For example, "183 Concord Street" instead of "183 Concord Place", is sufficient if there is only one street named "Concord" in the city. A search warrant directed against a hotel, motel, apartment house, or other multiple occupancy structure, must describe the particular room or subunit to be searched with sufficient definiteness to exclude a search of other units. For example, the description is insufficient if it describes the premises only by the street number of the building. However, the description may be sufficient if the search warrant adequately identifies the name of the occupant of the subunit intended.

A search warrant for the search of a *person* satisfies the constitutional requirements of particularity if the person is described in such a manner that he may be identified with reasonable certainty. For example, a search warrant describing a person merely as "John Doe" does not describe the person with sufficient particularity. However, the description is sufficient if there is an adequate physical description of the person and a description of the precise location at which he can be found. (**Note:** Where several locations are known to be occupied or controlled by the same person, the general rule is that separate warrants are *not* required; a single warrant may validly cover the several places.)

A search warrant for the search of a *thing* (property) satisfies the constitutional requirements of particularity if the thing is sufficiently described that it may be identified with reasonable certainty. For example, a description in a search warrant of a car to be searched or seized is sufficiently particular if it enables the officer, with reasonable certainty, to identify the car. The purpose of requiring a particular description of the property to be seized is to insure that the property taken is not left to the discretion of the police officers conducting the search.

4. *Issuance of Warrant* — Warrants may be issued only by a neutral and detached judge (magistrate). It is unconstitutional for federal or state prosecutors and policemen to issue search warrants. Statutes which permit law enforcement officers to issue search warrants violate the 4th and 14th Amendments. For example, a district attorney cannot issue a search warrant. (**Note:** Where there is a *mistake* in the warrant, only a judicial officer may alter, modify, or correct the warrant.)

5. *Execution of Warrant* — The process of carrying out a search or seizure under the direction of a search warrant is generally referred to as "executing" or "serving" the warrant. A search warrant may be executed only by the officers to whom it is directed. However, other persons may aid the officer if he requires it, and if the officer is present and acting in the execution of the warrant. A search made pursuant to a warrant, and seizures made during that search, must not only comply with procedural requirements, but must also strictly comply with all the directions contained in the warrant. For example, a search of a place which is not described in a search warrant is equivalent to searching without a warrant and is an unreasonable search under the 4th Amendment.

The seizure of "things" not specifically described in the search warrant is unlawful *unless* the items are (1) instrumentalities or fruits of crime, (2) contraband, or (3) evidence which is connected to criminal behavior. Items which are not contraband, stolen, or dangerous in themselves, and which are omitted from the description in the search warrant, may **not** be seized. Officers executing a search warrant, having found the thing or things listed in the warrant, may not lawfully continue to search for and seize additional evidence of the same crime. However, it is *not* a violation of the 4th Amendment for the officer to seize things not described in the warrant if such items are discovered inadvertently by the officer, in "plain view", and in the course of a proper execution of the warrant.

Federal rules require an officer taking property pursuant to a valid search warrant to give a copy of the warrant and a receipt to the person from whom the property was taken, or to leave the copy and receipt at the place from which the property was taken. Federal rules also require that a search warrant must be served in the daytime unless the judge (magistrate), by a specific provision in the warrant, authorizes its execution at night "for reasonable cause shown". However, a search which is properly begun in the daytime will not be invalidated merely because it continues into the night. (**Note:** The federal rule now expressly defines "daytime" as the hours between 6 o'clock a.m. and 10 o'clock p.m. local time.)

a. ***Knock and announce rule***—The general rule is that an officer executing a search warrant **must** give notice of his identity, notice of his authority, and announce his purpose before entering the premises. If the officer fails to comply with these conditions, the search is unlawful. This is the so-called "knock and announce" rule. The officer may open a door or window in order to execute the warrant only *after* he has given such notice and announcement. The officer need *not* announce his purpose before conducting an otherwise authorized search if such an announcement would endanger the officer or third persons, would provoke the escape of the suspect, or would permit the destruction of the things sought under the warrant.

D. EXCEPTIONS: NO WARRANT REQUIRED

1. *Exigent Circumstances (Critical or Urgent)*—A warrant is not required where officers have probable cause for the search or seizure *and* "exigent circumstances" exist which make it impractical to obtain a warrant. An exigent circumstance is where there is reasonable basis for believing that delaying a search in order to obtain a warrant

would endanger the physical safety of the officer or of third persons, or endanger the success of the search.

The U.S. Supreme Court has also held that police officers may search a dwelling without a warrant where they are *responding* to an "emergency" or where they are in "hot pursuit" of a fleeing felon. Where officers are not responding to an emergency (e.g., such as the sound of a shot and a cry for help) there must be critical or urgent circumstances to justify the absence of a warrant. (**Note:** When officers enter a dwelling and discover the person they are seeking, they are then justified in extending the scope of their search to the remainder of the dwelling, but only for the limited purpose of assuring themselves that no hostile and possibly dangerous persons are hiding in other rooms.)

2. *The "Plain View" Rule*—The plain view rule provides that it is **not** a "search" merely to observe what is in plain view (e.g., weapons, items dropped or discarded by fleeing suspects, drug paraphanalia, etc.). An otherwise valid search does not become unreasonable merely because of the observation and seizure of objects falling in the "plain view" of an officer who has a right to be in a position for such observation. In other words, the plain view rule applies *only* when a valid search is in progress; it does *not* apply when the officers are making an improper search.

An item can only be seized under the plain view rule if the officer has probable cause to believe that the item is subject to seizure and the officer inadvertently came across it and could see it while conducting a **valid** search. Any *material* evidence discovered may properly be seized, even if it is not the item for which the officer is searching. However, not every item lying within an area that may be searched may be seized; there must be some *connection* (nexus) between the items seized and a specific criminal activity. For example, the "fruits" and instruments of crime are, by their very nature, subject to seizure because they are things which constitute "evidence" of a crime.

So long as the observation, per se, is made by an officer

47

who has a right to be where he is, and encompasses only that which is in plain view, the fact that the observation was made by the use of binoculars or with a flashlight or searchlight will *not* transform it into a "search" or "seizure" within the meaning of the 4th Amendment. (**Note:** Officers may not deliberately *delay* an arrest until an arrestee is inside the premises in order to give the officers an opportunity to observe what is inside; in such circumstances, the officer's entry into the premises is unlawful.)

3. *"Stop and Frisk" Procedure*—The so-called stop and frisk procedure provides that when police officers believe a person is acting suspiciously and is likely to be armed, the officers may make an on-the-street stop, interrogation, and pat-down for **weapons.** Under such conditions a warrant is *not* necessary.

A "stop" is a **brief** detention of a person at the location where he is found for purposes of investigation in order to ascertain additional facts upon which to decide whether or not to arrest such person. Neither probable cause nor a warrant is required. The officer need only have some objective basis for believing that the person has been or is about to engage in criminal activity. The permissible scope of a "stop" does not include detention and interrogation for an extended period of time where the officers have no complaint or report of a crime, have never seen the suspect before, and have not observed him engaging in unlawful conduct.

The term "frisk" is generally defined to mean running the hand over the outer surfaces of the suspect's clothing. It is often referred to as a "pat-down". A person may be frisked **only** if the officer has some objective basis for fearing for his own physical safety or that of others who are nearby. Where the officer omits the pat-down from the outside and merely flips open the suspect's coat on the suspicion that the suspect is hiding something, the search becomes exploratory and is *not* within the proper scope of the stop and frisk procedure. A more intensive search may be made *only* if the frisk reveals further evidence that the suspect has a weapon. In other words, a frisk is **not** a search.

Where a stop and frisk procedure is justified, the frisk must be limited to that which is necessary for the discovery of weapons which might be used to harm the officer or others nearby. The officer need not be absolutely certain that the individual is armed. The issue is whether a reasonably prudent man under the circumstances would be warranted in the belief that his safety or that of others was in danger. However, if the officer has specific information that the suspect has a weapon and the specific location of the weapon, he may immediately search for it without conducting a preliminary frisk. (**Note:** If the suspect has not been taken into custody, the officer may not make a "full" body search.)

a.   *Airline passengers* — A frisk by a United States marshall of an airline passenger suspected of being a potential hijacker cannot intrude beyond the legitimate scope of a search for *weapons*. Any other fruits of such a search are inadmissible in a subsequent criminal proceeding. The frisk of airline passengers is justified because of the substantial interest in preserving the safety of air travel to the public by preventing hijacking.

The following procedures meet the 4th Amendment requirements under the stop and frisk exception to the warrant requirement, *provided* all of the steps are properly carried out: (1) the passenger is "focused upon" by airline employees because he meets a prescribed "profile" in which his characteristics match the characteristics of known hijackers; (2) the passenger, in walking along the passageway leading to the airplane, triggers a response by a magnetometer; (3) the passenger is then interviewed by airline personnel or by a U.S. marshall; (4) the passenger must be requested to walk through the magnetometer again; and (5) if the passenger again sets off the magnetometer while denying the possession of any metal, he may then be frisked by the U.S. marshall; if he refuses to walk through the magnetometer again, he must be released, but may be denied access to the airplane. (**Note:** Warrantless searches of

49

airline passengers are generally upheld on the basis of the consent of the passenger.)

4. *Incident to Lawful Arrest* — A search which is incident to a legal arrest may be made *without* a warrant. Whenever the police make a lawful arrest, they may make a contemporaneous search of the person arrested *and* the area under his **immediate control** for weapons or evidence which may be destroyed. A search incident to an arrest may extend to the portable personal effects in the immediate possession of the arrestee (e.g., a wallet). Similarly, all *companions* of the arrestee within the immediate vicinity who are capable of accomplishing a harmful assault upon the arresting officer may be "frisked" (not searched) in order to give assurance that they do not have weapons.

A search incident to an arrest may not extend to other rooms or even other areas within the same room, unless it is within the immediate control ("area of reach") of the person arrested. For example, a locked locker in a bus terminal may not be opened and its contents may not be seized as an incident to the arrest of the person renting the locker. Similarly, a suitcase may not be searched where it is not within the area of the arrestee's immediate control at the time of the arrest. [**Note:** A warrantless search may extend beyond the area within the arrestee's immediate control if there are special circumstances which pose an immediate *public* hazard (explosives).]

The discovery during a search incident to an arrest of a totally unrelated object which provides grounds for prosecution of a crime different from that for which the accused was arrested does *not* invalidate the search. (**Note:** The police may, when probable cause for arrest exists, enter a house without a warrant for the purpose of making that arrest, but may not conduct a search or seizure beyond that which falls within the narrow limits "incident" to the arrest.)

A person arrested is subject to a "full" search of his outer body provided there is no illegal detention or interrogation. For example, the police may scrape under a

50

suspect's fingernails if they have probable cause to arrest him, reason to believe that evidence of guilt will be found by such action, and reason to believe that delaying the search will enable the suspect to destroy the evidence. (**Note:** A search or seizure made without a warrant cannot be justified as incident to an arrest unless the *arrest* was constitutionally valid.)

a. *Incident to "traffic" arrest* — An arresting officer may search a vehicle in which a person is *arrested*, provided the search is contemporaneous with, and incident to the arrest. Evidence of a crime which is in "plain view" in the passenger compartment of the vehicle is not subject to the 4th Amendment protection and may be "seized". In other words, it does not constitute an unlawful search for a police officer to seize contraband, instrumentalities or other evidence of crime which is in plain view at the time of the arrest. Where the arresting officers have *probable cause* to believe that they will find an instrumentality or evidence of a crime *before* they begin their search, they may search for weapons and concealable evidence only **within the reach** of the arrestee (e.g., within his immediate control). Thus, a search of the trunk of a vehicle is unreasonable if the arrestee could not, at that time, have reached into the trunk.

Where the officers have probable cause to believe that the arrestee is *armed and dangerous*, the officers may also frisk the arrestee for weapons under the "stop and frisk" exception to the warrant requirement. [**Note:** Where a person has *abandoned* personal property which is subsequently acquired by the police, it does *not* constitute an unreasonable search and seizure (e.g., where a paper bag has been thrown away from a vehicle by a motorist stopped for a traffic offense).]

In a *minority* of states searches incident to traffic arrests may be justified on the basis of a "furtive gesture" *provided* there is either additional suspicious information (e.g., a delay by the suspect in stopping his car) or the traffic arrest occurred at night. In other words, a mere "furtive gesture" alone (e.g., merely leaning over to place some object beneath the seat of a car) will *not* constitute probable cause for a search.

b. *Search of "moving" vehicle* — A vehicle is considered moving if it is either in movement, or is stopped, but ready to move (e.g., the motor is running). A "moving" vehicle may be searched without a warrant whenever there is *probable cause* to believe the vehicle contains something subject to seizure. To delay the search in order to obtain a warrant would permit the vehicle to be quickly moved out of the locality or jurisdiction in which the warrant must be sought. In other words, the evidence may never be found again if there is a delay while a warrant is obtained.

c. *Search of "moveable" vehicle* — A vehicle is "moveable" if it is stopped, but is in reasonable working order (e.g., can be driven). A moveable vehicle cannot be searched without a warrant unless there is sufficient probable cause. The mere fact that a vehicle is in reasonable working order and moveable does *not*, per se, provide sufficient probable cause to search the vehicle without a warrant. (**Note:** Where "exigent" circumstances exist, a moveable vehicle may be searched without a warrant.)

There is a split of authority as to whether police may conduct an *inventory search* of vehicles taken into custody. An "inventory search" is the taking and holding of all the contents of the vehicle incident to its impoundment and storage. Some states permit no such search; the vehicle must be sealed. Other states permit a full inspection. Still other states authorize a limited inventory inspection, but do not permit intrusion into items found in the vehicle (e.g., suitcases, boxes, etc.).

5. *Information From an Informant* — The utilization of un-

dercover agents or informers does not, per se, constitute a "search" or "seizure". An officer may rely on information from an informant when making a search without a warrant, provided the informant's statement is reasonably *corroborated* by other matters within the officer's knowledge. Using an informer to gain access to information voluntarily disclosed to the informer (but in ignorance of the fact that he is an informer) is *not* a search within the meaning of the 4th Amendment. For example, information obtained by an informer posing as a purchaser of narcotics in order to enter the seller's home for the purpose of making a transaction does not constitute an unlawful search.

6. *Border Searches* — An individual, his effects, and his vehicle may be searched at the international border of the United States in order to determine whether he is an improperly entered alien, whether other improperly entered aliens are concealed in his vehicle, and whether he has any items improperly brought across the international border. No warrant is necessary; "mere suspicion" is sufficient.

Strip searches (requiring the suspect to disrobe) and body cavity searches may also be conducted without a warrant at the international border of the United States. However, more than "mere suspicion" is required to support such searches; there must be a "clear indication" that items subject to seizure will be found.

E. EXCLUSIONARY RULE

1. *Illegally Obtained Evidence Excluded* — The exclusionary rule excludes evidence obtained from a search and seizure which is unreasonable under the 4th Amendment. In the early case of *Weeks v. U.S. (1914)* the Supreme Court established the so-called "exclusionary rule" by providing that any evidence obtained from an **illegal** search and seizure by *federal* officers is **not** admissible against an accused in a criminal prosecution in a *federal* court whenever a timely objection to the use of such evidence has been made by the accused. Oral evidence of what was found or seen by the officers during

the illegal search and **verbal declarations** made by the accused during the illegal search are also inadmissible and must be excluded.

The Supreme Court subsequently held that evidence obtained by a search and seizure in violation of the 4th Amendment is also inadmissible in **state** courts as a matter of due process and equal protection. [*Mapp v. Ohio (1961)*] Thus, *all* states are now required to follow the exclusionary rule. In other words, evidence illegally obtained must be excluded from criminal prosecutions in **both** the state and federal courts. (**Note:** In 1966 the Supreme Court held that evidence obtained during custodial interrogation in violation of the 5th Amendment protection against self-incrimination also falls within the exclusionary rule and is inadmissible. [*Miranda v. Arizona (1966)*].)

The exclusionary rule is limited to prohibiting the government from using evidence against the accused which has been obtained from him illegally. It does *not* prohibit the government from using such evidence to **impeach** an accused's voluntary testimony. For example, a confession inadmissible on *Miranda* grounds will be admissible if the *sole* purpose is to discredit the testimony of the accused. Similarly, the exclusionary rule does *not* apply if an illegal search is made by a *private* individual acting on his **own** initiative. For example, a trespasser (one who is wrongfully present upon the premises of another) may testify as to those facts observed by him while trespassing. [**Note:** If a private person commits an illegal search and seizure as the *agent* of public officials, his testimony will be *excluded* (inadmissible) under the exclusionary rule.]

2. *"Fruits of the Poisonous Tree"* —Under the exclusionary rule not only must evidence directly seized in an unlawful search be excluded, but all evidence *derived* from an illegal search or seizure must also be excluded. That is, all evidence **indirectly** acquired as a result of information derived from illegally obtained evidence is inadmissible. This is the so-called "fruit of the poisonous tree" doc-

trine. In other words, if illegally obtained evidence is the "source" (e.g., the poisonous tree) of information which leads to additional evidence (e.g., the fruits), the additional evidence must be excluded. For example, evidence discovered as a result of specific leads obtained from an unlawful search is inadmissible.

The "fruit of the poisonous tree" doctrine extends only to facts which were *actually discovered* as a result of investigating a particular crime. As a general rule courts will not make an inquiry or investigate into the source of the evidence or the means by which it was obtained; the issue must be raised by the *accused*.

3. *Electronic Surveillance (Wiretapping and Eavesdropping)* — Any form of mechanical or electronic surveillance that violates a reasonable expectation of privacy constitutes a search protected by the 4th Amendment. The use of such devices to overhear private conversations is prohibited unless there is *prior* authorization pursuant to a *court order*.

    a.   *Federal Communications Act*—The Federal Communication Act prohibits the interception of any communication, and the divulging or publishing of the contents, substance, purport, effect, or meaning of such intercepted communication to any person unless authorized by the sender. The term "interception" refers only to the *physical interruption* (tapping) of wire or oral communications ("wiretapping"). In the absence of authority from the sender, the government cannot intercept wire or oral communications unless it has prior authorization from a federal court of competent jurisdiction. [**Note:** The Act applies **only** to the tapping of telephone and telegraph lines; it does *not* apply to mechanical or electronic *eavesdropping* (e.g., "overhearing" a statement).]

The Supreme Court has recently held that the 4th Amendment protects people, not places, and that **every** electronic eavesdropping upon private conversations (including wiretapping) is a *search and seizure* within the protection of the 4th Amendment. [*Katz v. United States (1967)*] The court held that any evidence obtained by the use or installation of mechanical or electronic eavesdropping devices *without judicial authorization* constitutes an unreasonable search and seizure and must be *excluded*. Similarly, the "fruits" of unauthorized electronic eavesdropping are also inadmissible.

Thus, the 4th Amendment applies not only to the seizure of tangible items, but also to the seizure (recording) of oral statements (intangible items) obtained by means of electronic listening devices. In other words, the right to privacy and security under the 4th Amendment are as clearly invaded when the police make a search for "intangible" property *without authorization* as they are when the police make a search for "tangible" property *without a warrant*.

Under the Katz decision the scope of the 4th Amendment protection applies to the *use* or *installation* of any electronic eavesdropping device (including wiretapping); it does *not* depend upon the mere presence or absence of a "physical" intrusion into any given enclosure. For example, in the absence of judicial authority to do so, merely "attaching" an electronic listening device to the outside wall of a telephone booth and recording the words spoken by the occupant of the booth constitutes an unreasonable search and seizure.

Electronic eavesdropping is permitted **only** with advanced authorization by a *neutral judge* (1) upon a showing of *probable cause*; (2) under *precise limitations* (the particular conversation to be overheard must be described, the persons making them must be named, and the surveillance must be limited to a short period of time); and (3) under *appropriate safeguards* (provision for termination of the surveillance and notifying the judge of all that has been seized). [**Note:** Evidence obtained by mere eavesdropping without a mechanical or electronic listening device (e.g., "overhearing"), if relevant, does *not* come within the exclusionary rule; it is not an "unreasonable" search or seizure.]

F. MOTION TO SUPPRESS

1. *Separate Hearing on Admissibility* — A court will not grant an "injunction" to prevent evidence obtained by means of an illegal search and seizure from being used in a criminal trial; the accused must seek a motion to suppress in the trial court. A motion to supress evidence obtained by an illegal search and seizure, and to direct its return, is the proper remedy to exclude such evidence from the trial. If the accused can prove that the evidence was obtained by an illegal search and seizure, the evidence will be suppressed. However, the general rule is that the motion to suppress the admission of evidence must be made *before* trial. In other words, it is a **pretrial** motion.

   When the accused files a motion to suppress, he is entitled to have a **separate hearing** (1) on the issue of admissibility, (2) prior to its being submitted to the jury, and (3) out of the presence of the jury. The accused must be permitted to testify at the hearing regarding the inadmissibility and suppression of such evidence. (**Note:** A motion to suppress is not necessary where the accused has no knowledge of the facts which would enable him to file the motion.)

   The order of the court regarding a motion to suppress is generally considered final and may be appealed to the highest available state court and, in the event of an adverse determination, to the U.S. Supreme Court. Evidence which has been suppressed will generally be returned to the owner *unless* the possession of the evidence constitutes a crime and the repossession of it would subject the owner to criminal penalties.

2. *Standing* — An accused may challenge evidence on the grounds of the exclusionary rule **only** if he has "standing" to do so. In order to have standing to object to evidence obtained by an illegal search and seizure (or custodial interrogation), an accused must have been the *victim* (e.g., the one against whom the search or interrogation was directed). However, the accused must prove that he has a *legal* interest in the premises searched or the prop-

57

erty seized. That is, an accused does not have standing to object to an illegal search and seizure unless (1) he is the owner of the premises or property, or (2) he is lawfully on the premises or property when it is searched.

Any person lawfully on the premises when a search occurs has standing to challenge the legality of the search if the "fruits" of the search are proposed to be used against him in a criminal prosecution. (**Note:** An accused has "automatic" standing to challenge the means by which an item was obtained if he has been charged with illegal possession of that item.)

§4. PRIVILEGE AGAINST SELF-INCRIMINATION

A. GUARANTEED BY 5TH AND 14TH AMENDMENTS

1. *Cannot Be Compelled To Be Witness Against Self*—The 5th Amendment to the U.S. Constitution provides that a person who has been accused of a crime has a privilege *not* to be **compelled** to give testimony against himself which could incriminate him in the crime. The privilege against self-incrimination contained in the 5th Amendment to the Constitution has been "incorporated" into the 14th Amendment and applies to state actions. The privilege against self-incrimination is also contained in most state constitutions.

   The privilege applies to both civil and criminal proceedings whenever the accused or a witness *might* be subjected to criminal responsibility. Testimony sought as a part of a legitimate *noncriminal* (civil) matter is also privileged provided such testimony would tend to incriminate under state or federal criminal law. For example, the privilege may be invoked in an administrative hearing or congressional investigation. However, if the accused (or a witness) responds to the questions put to him instead of claiming the privilege, he **cannot** later raise the defense of self-incrimination and bar that evidence from a criminal prosecution against him. (**Note:** A corporation may *not* assert the privilege; only natural persons may do so.)

   The privilege against self-incrimination applies only to a compelled **oral** examination or its equivalent (e.g., written statements or confessions); it does *not* protect against other forms of examination such as compelling an accused to exhibit his person. In other words, only **testimonial** evidence of a communicative nature is included in the 5th Amendment privilege.

There is **no inference of guilt** solely because an accused has invoked the privilege against self-incrimination. A person has the right to assert the privilege and remain *silent* without suffering any penalty for such silence. Where an accused fails to testify, comment by the prosecution regarding the accused's silence, or instructions by the court that such silence is evidence of guilt, is prohibited.

An accused does **not** have to take the stand as a witness against himself. In such a case, the prosecutor *cannot* make any statements to the jury about why the accused did not take the stand. A person may also invoke or "take" the 5th Amendment when called before a Congressional Committee or when called as a witness in another case. When a person is merely a witness in a case, he does not have to answer questions which may incriminate him. For example, a person who may have witnessed or been involved in a crime need not answer questions at another's trial concerning that crime, or before a Grand Jury which is investigating that crime. However, if a person has been granted *immunity* from prosecution for the crime in return for his testimony, he **can** be compelled to testify.

When federal or state statutory requirements create a *substantial and real hazard* of incrimination by complying with such requirements, the privilege against self-incrimination may be asserted in order to avoid prosecution for failure to comply. The following have been held to constitute such a hazard; registration of participation in a particular business enterprise (e.g., registering the transfer of marijuana); possession of certain property (e.g., registration of a sawed-off shotgun); or by payment of taxes for engaging in certain occupational activity (e.g., payment of a wagering tax).

(**Note:** When *insanity* is interposed as a defense, an examination of the accused by experts for the purpose of determining his mental condition in regard thereto does **not** violate the accused's constitutional privilege against self-incrimination.)

2. *Compelled Self-incriminating Physical Act Not Prohibited* — Requiring that the accused disclose his physical characteristics or habits does not violate the privilege against self-incrimination, since the evidence is *not* "testimonial". For example, an accused may be compelled to stand up for the purpose of identification. Similarly, the privilege against self-incrimination does not apply to *physical* evidence which may be revealed by compelling the accused to exhibit himself in any manner in which an ordinary person is commonly seen in public. For example, the court, the jury, and the witnesses testifying in the case, all have the right to observe the appearance of the accused.

The general rule is that it is *not* a violation of the privilege against self-incrimination to compel the accused to perform an act which is outside the court or out of the presence of the jury; a witness may testify as to such act because the evidence is *not* "testimonial". For example, an accused may be compelled to try on or model clothing, have his footprints or shoes compared to tracks at the scene of the crime, put a handkerchief over part of his face, appear in a police lineup, assume certain poses, be photographed, speak for voice identification, or give a handwriting sample. (**Note:** Most courts hold that the accused may *not* be compelled to perform any such "evidence producing" physical act *in open court* if it might aid in establishing the accused's *guilt*.)

Similarly, it is *not* a violation of the privilege against self-incrimination to compel the accused to submit to scientific or medical analysis of his body outside the court and away from the jury. For example, the accused may be compelled to submit to a physical examination of his body; to a blood, urine, or breath test in order to measure the amount of alcohol in his blood or urine; or to an analysis and comparison of his blood with blood found at the scene of the crime, or with the victim's blood. A physician may testify as to his findings from such analysis or examination, even though made *without* the accused's consent because such evidence is considered "physical" and *not* testimonial.

3. *Immunity From Prosecution*—In the **majority** of jurisdictions, statutes expressly provide for *immunity* from prosecution to a **witness** who has been compelled to give testimony which would incriminate him under either state or federal criminal law. In other words, a witness who has been granted immunity from federal and state use of any compelled testimony (and the "fruits" of that testimony) *can* be compelled to answer questions; however, such testimony (or its fruits) may **not** be used in any federal or state criminal prosecution of the witness. Thus, a grant of state immunity is a grant of federal immunity and vice versa.

The purpose of immunity provisions is (1) to induce criminals or their confederates to testify against each other in order to obtain evidence which would otherwise be unobtainable because of the Constitutional privilege against self-incrimination, and (2) to protect every person who gives testimony which would directly or indirectly be helpful to the prosecution in securing an indictment or a conviction.

The established practice in most jurisdictions is not to prosecute an *accessory* (or accomplice) who has testified for the government in the expectation of immunity from prosecution. The rationale is that an accessory has an "equitable" right to the same immunity from prosecution as that which is provided to other witnesses for the state. However, the fact that an accessory has given testimony of an incriminating nature does *not* (in the absence of a statute so providing) entitle him to claim immunity from prosecution as a matter of *right*.

B. CONFESSIONS (ADMISSION OF GUILT)

1. *Must Be Voluntary*—A confession is an *admission* by an accused, without any exculpating statement or explana-

tion, that he is **guilty** of the crime with which he is charged. It is *not* an admission of a fact or circumstance from which guilt may be inferred. In other words, a statement which admits the commission of the act charged, but which also gives a legal justification or excuse, is not a confession.

The confession of an accused is admissible in evidence against him only if it was freely and **voluntarily** made; that is, without duress, fear, or compulsion in its inducement and with full knowledge of its nature and consequences. For example, a voluntary confession which has been reduced to writing is admissible in evidence, *provided* it was signed by the accused or affirmed by the accused as correct. An **involuntary** confession comes within the exclusionary rule and is *inadmissible* in evidence against the accused in both federal and state courts. A conviction obtained by means of an involuntary confession deprives the accused of his freedom without due process of law. A confession is involuntary if it has been *induced* by hope or promise of benefit, reward, or immunity, or *coerced* by force, violence, fear, or threats.

a. *Judicial confession*—A judicial confession is a plea of guilty made before a committing *judge* or *in open court*. A judicial confession voluntarily made is admissible in evidence.

b. *Extrajudicial confession*—An extrajudicial confession is one which is *not* made before a judge or in open court. Extrajudicial confessions are admissible in evidence against the accused **only** if made voluntarily (without coercion or improper inducements) and not in violation of the Constitutional rights to counsel and to remain silent.

2. *Must Be Corroborated*—The general rule is that a **voluntary** extrajudicial confession of guilt by one accused of crime, uncorroborated by any other evidence, is *not* sufficient to warrant or sustain a conviction; there must be *corroboration*. In other words, a conviction will be upheld **only** when there is independent evidence of the corpus delecti (e.g., that someone committed a crime to

which the accused has confessed). (**Note:** A conviction will *not* be upheld if it is based, in whole or in part, on an *involuntary* confession, regardless of its truth or falsity, even if there is corroborative evidence to support the conviction.)

The general rule is that the voluntary confession of a *codefendant* made after the commission of a crime *cannot* be admitted against another unless it was made in the other's presence and assented to by him. However, it may be admitted against the confessing codefendant. Similarly, a confession by a *third person* that he, and not the accused, committed the crime is *inadmissible* as evidence to acquit the accused.

3. *Promise or Inducement (Involuntary)* — The confession of an accused which is induced or influenced by promises which hold out a hope of benefit or reward is *involuntary*. It is not admissible in evidence since it creates a fair probability of its untrustworthiness as testimony. However, the inducements of benefit or reward which will exclude a confession must be *directly* applied by a *third person*; that is, it must not arise from the mere operation of the accused person's own independent reasoning. For example, the promise of a "collateral" benefit if the accused will confess does *not* make the confession involuntary (e.g., a promise of future employment or to divide a reward for the capture of the guilty person). Similarly, a promise of benefits which are moral, religious, or spiritual in nature do *not* make the confession involuntary.

A confession induced by a promise of leniency, clemency, immunity, or to free the accused in return for his confession, is deemed to be *involuntary*. In other words, a confession obtained on the assurance that the accused will not be prosecuted, or that his punishment will be lessened, is *not* admissible in evidence against him. (**Note:** A confession is not involuntary merely because the accused was told that it would be better for him to tell the truth, unless threats or promises are also involved. The mere suggestion to an accused that he confess will not exclude a confession; it is only advice, and not a threat.)

A voluntary confession of crime by an accused who is of *less than normal intelligence* is admissible, provided the subnormality has not deprived him of the capacity to understand the meaning and effect of the confession. Similarly, a confession is admissible even though the person making it is a *minor*. In determining the voluntariness and admissibility of a minor's confession, the court will consider the age of the minor, his personal condition, intelligence, lack of intelligence, character, situation, disposition, experience, etc.

4. *Force or Threats of Force (Involuntary)* — A confession which is induced by force, violence, or fear directed at the accused is **involuntary** and not admissible in evidence against him. In order to render a confession involuntary and inadmissible because it was induced by fear, the fear must have been caused by outside pressure brought to bear on the accused, as distinguished from fear arising from his own imagination. (**Note:** *Trickery* or *deception* in obtaining a confession, such as pretending to possess evidence against the accused, does **not** make the confession involuntary and inadmissible. For example, a confession obtained by an informer disguised as a fellow prisoner is voluntary and admissible.)

a. *Delay in arraignment (federal courts)* — In *federal* courts a delay in arraignment will render a confession obtained during the period of such delay involuntary and inadmissible unless: (1) such confession is found by the trial judge to have been voluntary, (2) the weight to be given the confession is left to the jury, and (3) the confession was made or given by the accused within six hours immediately following his arrest or other detention. The federal rule is **not** binding on *state* courts. State courts generally hold that a mere delay in arraignment does not render a confession involuntary and inadmissible, although it is a fact to be taken into consideration in the determination of whether a confession was voluntarily made.

b. *"Third degree" confessions* — A confession obtained

without inducement or coercion, but under circumstances which "overbear" the accused's *will* as to whether or not to confess, is *involuntary*. "Third degree" questioning is a process of *interrogation* which is so prolonged and unremitting, especially when accompanied by deprivation of refreshment, rest, or relief, that it results in "extortion" of an involuntary confession (e.g., obtaining a confession by making the accused stand facing a wall with his hands up throughout the night). Confessions obtained by "third degree" questioning are involuntary and inadmissible because such methods necessarily produce a *coerced* confession.

C. CONFESSION DURING "CUSTODIAL INTERROGATION"

1. ***Miranda* Warnings (*Right to Counsel and To Remain Silent*)**—In 1966 the U.S. Supreme Court held that confessions or statements made during **custodial interrogation** of the accused may *not* be used in a criminal case by the prosecution unless there were effective procedural safeguards securing the privilege against self-incrimination. [*Miranda v. Arizona* (1966)] The *Miranda* decision applies only where there is custody **and** interrogation. "Custody" consists of depriving another of his freedom by some physical detention. For example, not only may a person be in custody at a police station, but he may also be in custody when detained in his own bedroom. "Interrogation" consists of asking questions *and* attempting to stimulate an incriminating statement. Thus, "custodial interrogation" is questioning initiated by law enforcement officers after a person has been taken into custody (or otherwise deprived of his freedom) which stimulates such person to incriminate himself in a crime.

Under *Miranda* the accused must be **warned** that (1) he has a right to *remain silent*; (2) that any statement he does make *may be used as evidence against him*; and (3) that he has a right to the *presence of an attorney*, either retained or appointed. The opportunity to exercise all of these rights must be afforded to the accused throughout the interrogation. If the warning does not satisfy these three rquirements, the confession or statement is involuntary and inadmissible, even if the accused was aware he had such rights. In other words, mere knowledge of his rights does not constitute a waiver of the *Miranda* warnings; the accused must be **actually** warned of his rights.

Any **waiver** of his rights by the accused *before* such warnings are given is *invalid*. Only **after** such warnings have been given, **and** an opportunity to exercise such rights have been permitted, may the accused (or suspect) knowingly and intelligently waive these particular rights and agree to answer questions or make a statement or confession. In other words, in the *absence* of warnings *and* waiver, evidence obtained as a result of custodial interrogation **cannot** be used against the accused in a criminal proceeding.

Volunteered statements or confessions made to the police without interrogation are *not* barred by the 5th Amendment privilege against self-incrimination or by *Miranda* and are admissible in evidence. The fact that the accused was illegally detained when a confession was made does not make it involuntary unless the illegal detention induced or contributed to the obtaining of the confession. In other words, a person may talk to the police without benefit of warnings and counsel, but he *cannot* be interrogated without benefit of warnings and counsel.

The right to have **counsel** present at the interrogation is *indispensable* to the protection of the 5th Amendment privilege against self-incrimination. It is necessary to warn the accused (or suspect) not only that he has the right to consult an attorney, but also that if he is indigent, a lawyer will be appointed to represent him. If an individual held for interrogation by police states that he wants an attorney, the interrogation **must** cease until an attorney is *present*; and the individual must be given an opportunity to confer with the attorney and to have him present during any subsequent questioning.

The right to remain silent at the interrogation is also *indispensable* to the protection of the 5th Amendment privilege against self-incrimination. A valid waiver will **not** be presumed merely from the silence of the accused after warnings are given or merely from the fact that a confession was in fact eventually obtained. Also, the fact that the accused answered some questions or volunteered some statements on his own does not deprive him of the right to remain silent and refrain from answering any further questions until he has consulted with an attorney and thereafter consents to the question.

Statements made without *Miranda* warnings immediately after an arrest are inadmissible; however, if the accused is temporarily released (recognizance or bail) and **subsequently** makes a voluntary self-incriminating statement, such subsequent statement is *admissible*. After the *Miranda* warnings have been given, a confession made while the accused is under arrest or in the custody of a police officer is admissible provided it is voluntary.

5. RIGHT TO SPEEDY TRIAL

A. GUARANTEED BY 6TH AND 14TH AMENDMENTS

1. *Pretrial Prejudice To Rights Of Accused* — The 6th Amendment to the U.S. Constitution provides that the accused has a right to a **speedy** trial in all *federal* criminal prosecutions. The 6th Amendment has been "incorporated" into the 14th Amendment so that the right to a speedy trial is also guaranteed in *state* criminal prosecutions. The same right is also expressed in most state constitutions. The right to a speedy trial does *not* include the right to a speedy appeal; its purpose is to prevent pretrial oppression of the accused and undue delay in bringing him to trial. [**Note:** If a trial is too speedy and denies the accused an opportunity to prepare, it may violate the Constitutional guarantee of due process (fair trial). For example, an accused is entitled to notice of the date of trial in sufficient time to have his witnesses present in court.]

The burden is on the accused to show that the state (through its prosecuting officers) caused the delay. If he cannot do so, the presumption is that the delay was caused by or with his own consent. Whether the right to a speedy trial has been denied depends upon the following: (1) whether or not the accused asserted his right to a speedy trial; (2) the length of delay; (3) who caused the delay (court system, prosecutor, or defense); (4) any justification for the delay; *and* (5) prejudice to the rights of the accused. [**Note:** The right to speedy trial is *not* violated by unavoidable delays (e.g., docket congestion; attempts of the accused to obtain "private" counsel.)]

The rights of the accused are deemed to be "prejudiced" when the delay has caused the accused to remain in jail for an undue amount of time while awaiting trial (e.g., prolonged pretrial incarceration); when it impairs the ability of the accused to prepare his case or to make a defense; or when the delay causes pretrial public suspicion of the accused regarding the untried criminal charges.

2. *As Soon As Possible After Arrest or Indictment*—The U.S. Constitution provides no specific time within which an accused must be brought to trial. However, in the **majority** of jurisdictions, statutes have been enacted which "implement" the constitutional right to speedy trial by providing that an accused must be discharged if not brought to trial within (1) a certain statutory period after arrest, or (2) a certain statutory period after indictment. In other words, the right to a speedy trial attaches when the accused has been arrested or formally charged. Although the right to a speedy trial can be violated by an unreasonable delay in the return of the indictment after the arrest has been made, the right to a speedy trial is *not* violated by a delay *between* the crime and the indictment (or the arrest, if it precedes the indictment).

Delaying an arrest does not deny the accused his right to a speedy trial unless it violates the Constitutional requirements of due process (fair trial). However, once an indictment (or some other formal charge) has been returned against a person, the right to speedy trial will be denied by an unreasonable delay in making the arrest. (**Note:** An accused is constitutionally entitled to a speedy trial on a *pending* charge, even if he is already imprisoned and serving a sentence for a different crime.)

The right to a speedy trial does not require a trial immediately upon the presentation of the indictment or upon the arrest since the prosecution must be permitted a reasonable time to prepare for the trial. The only remedy for a denial of the right to speedy trial is *dismissal* of the case. Such dismissal **must** be "with prejudice" to the prosecution; that is, the prosecution *cannot* subsequently reinstate the indictment and prosecute the accused. If the dismissal is "without prejudice" (e.g., the prosecution can be reinstated at any time), it denies the right to a speedy trial and the court must dismiss the case *on the merits*.

§6. RIGHT TO PUBLIC TRIAL

A. GUARANTEED BY 6TH AND 14TH (DUE PROCESS) AMENDMENTS

1. *Criminal Proceedings Only* — Virtually every state constitution guarantees the right to a public trial. In federal criminal prosecutions, the right to public trial is expressly protected by the 6th Amendment to the U.S. Constitution. The 6th Amendment does **not** apply to state prosecutions. However, denial of a public trial may be a denial of due process under the 5th and 14th Amendments.

   A public trial is generally defined as a trial at which the public is "free to attend" or which is "not secret". The right to a public trial applies to all stages of the trial; that is, the public cannot be arbitrarily excluded from any part of a trial. The guarantee of a public trial is used to restrain any abuse of judicial power or any attempt to use the courts as instruments of persecution. (**Note:** The constitutional right to a public trial applies to *criminal* proceedings **only**.)

   Where excessive outside influences deny the right to a fair and impartial trial, the court, in its discretion, may exclude the public from the trial. For example, if the trial is influenced by a carnival-like atmosphere, by mob psychology, or by the press and other mass media which continually disturb or influence the trial (e.g., interviewing prospective witnesses who disclose testimony), it is a denial of a fair and impartial trial which violates due process.

The court may also exclude the public in order to protect the rights of the parties and witnesses (e.g., sex cases), to preserve order and decorum in the courtroom, and for any other purpose which furthers the administration of justice. [**Note:** When the courtroom is too small to accommodate all those who wish to attend the trial, it is *not* a denial of due process (the right to a public trial) for the trial judge to limit the number of spectators in order to prevent overcrowding of the courtroom and disruption of the trial.]

§7. RIGHT TO AN IMPARTIAL JURY

A. GUARANTEED BY 6TH AND 14TH AMENDMENTS

1. *Essential to Fair Trial*—The 6th Amendment to the U.S. Constitution guarantees an accused the right to trial by an impartial jury in all federal prosecutions. The right to an impartial jury is essential to a fair trial as a matter of due process and is guaranteed in state criminal prosecutions by the due process clause of the 14th Amendment. (**Note:** The function of the judge during the trial is to rule on questions of *law;* the function of the jury during the trial is to determine questions of *fact*.)

Evidence against an accused must be presented to a jury in a public courtroom where there is judicial protection of the accused's right to confrontation, cross-examination, and counsel. Members of the jury must be insulated not only from the accused, but also from the prosecution and its witnesses. For example, if the prosecution or any of its witnesses discuss the trial or the accused's guilt with a member of the jury during the trial, the accused's right to due process is violated.

Juries are usually composed of twelve persons who are citizens of the United States, understand the English language, and reside within the court's jurisdiction. However, an accused does *not* have a Constitutional right to a jury of twelve. The general rule is that the jury need only be large enough to be free from outside attempts at intimidation, and to provide a "fair possibility" of being composed of a representative **cross-section** of the community.

The Constitutional right to trial by an impartial jury does *not* include the right to an unanimous verdict. However, under federal rules and in a **majority** of states, a jury's verdict must be *unanimous*. If all the jurors cannot agree (e.g., a "hung jury") the case against the accused must be dismissed and the accused must be released. However, such dismissal does *not* amount to an acquittal and the prosecution may, in its discretion, seek a new trial with a new jury. A **minority** of states permit verdicts which are not unanimous (e.g., verdict by 2/3 of jury). A less than unanimous verdict is **not** unconstitutional *unless* the accused's right to due process or equal protection is violated. For example, a nine to three majority verdict of guilt beyond a reasonable doubt does not violate due process or equal protection under the 5th and 14th Amendments.

2. *Discrimination In Selecting Jurors* —Jurors are generally selected from a list of persons eligible to vote in the county or district where the trial is being held. The general rule is that the composition of the jury cannot be grounds for a denial of due process or equal protection *unless* the jury was selected on a discriminatory basis. In other words, an accused has *no* right to a jury composed of his "equals" or his "peers". In order to void a conviction on the grounds of an impartial jury, the Supreme Court has held that the trial record must show that the exclusion of prospective jurors so affected the composition of the jury as to make it *prone* to pronounce a guilty verdict.

The **purposeful** exclusion of *prospective* jurors on "racial" grounds is discriminatory and requires a new trial as a matter of equal protection and due process of law. The general rule is that a jury is *not* impartial and the accused will be denied a fair trial if prospective jurors are selected from a *racially segregated* tax digest or voting list. (Note:Although an accused has a right to have blacks or women on the list from which jurors are called, there does **not** have to be a black person or a woman on the accused's *particular* jury.)

71

§8. RIGHT TO CONFRONT ACCUSER AND WITNESSES

A. GUARANTEED BY 6TH AND 14TH AMENDMENTS

1. *Opportunity To Cross–Examine (To Prevent Hearsay)* — The right of an accused to confront witnesses against him is a fundamental right essential to a fair trial. In federal criminal prosecutions, the 6th Amendment to the Constitution guarantees an accused the right to confront the witnesses against him (e.g., his accusers) in open court. The confrontation clause of the 6th Amendment has been specifically "incorporated" into the due process clause of the 14th Amendment by the Supreme Court so that the right of an accused to confront the witnesses against him is also guaranteed in state trials. (**Note:** Although the right of an accused to confront his accusers requires that he be present in the courtroom during the trial, the right to confrontation may be *restricted* if the conduct of the accused makes it impossible or too difficult to conduct the trial.)

   The primary purpose for the requirement of confrontation is to provide an opportunity to *cross–examine* the witnesses against the accused. The secondary purpose for the requirement of confrontation is to provide an opportunity for the judge and jury to see the witness' *demeanor* (personal appearance, conduct, deportment, etc.) while testifying.

2. *Trial Only* — The accused's right to be confronted by his accusers applies only to the actual trial itself; it does *not* apply to the preliminary hearing, arraignment, or any other preliminary proceeding. When an accused does not speak the English language, or does not understand it, the judge must appoint someone to interpret the testimony of the English speaking witnesses. A failure to provide an interpreter which in any manner hampers the accused in presenting his case to the jury is a denial of a fair and impartial trial and violates the right to due process.

   Statements which are not made at the trial are considered "hearsay" (unsubstantiated repetition or rumor) and are generally inadmissible. The rationale is that the accused has been denied the opportunity to cross-examine and confront the person making the statement. However, the general rule is that hearsay evidence *will* be admitted under the following conditions: (1) where the prosecution has made a good faith effort to obtain the "in court" testimony of the witness and has failed; *and* (2) where the accused has had a previous opportunity to cross-examine the witness as to such testimony. For example, testimony of a witness at a preliminary hearing is admissible at the trial if the *accused* had an adequate opportunity to cross-examine the witness at such preliminary hearing.

a. ***Disclosure of informer's identity***—The general rule is that the prosecution is *not* required to disclose the identity of an informer unless such disclosure is **material** to the accused's defense or to the disposition of the case (e.g., a fair and impartial trial). If the informer is merely the "source" of the information which provides probable cause to arrest the accused, the prosecution is *not* required to reveal the informer's identity. For example, if an informant obtained his information illegally by wiretapping, but was not a participant in the crime charged, the prosecution may withhold the identity of the informer because it has no bearing on the guilt or innocence of the accused. If the informant "participated" in the crime in any way (with or without the knowledge of law officers) the informer's identity must be disclosed since he may possess additional knowledge which could be material to the defense of the accused.

§9. RIGHT TO COUNSEL

A. GUARANTEED BY 6TH AND 14TH AMENDMENTS

1. *Essential to Fair Trial*—The 6th Amendment to the U.S. Constitution provides that in all criminal prosecutions the accused has the right to have the assistance of counsel for his defense. The Supreme Court has held that the Constitutional right to the assistance of counsel is *essential* to a fair and impartial trial of the accused as a matter of due process (5th and 14th Amendment). The accused's right

to counsel is also guaranteed under the constitutions of most states. The accused is entitled to be given a fair opportunity to obtain a private attorney of his own choice or, if the accused is "indigent", to have an attorney appointed by the court to act in his behalf. The accused's right to counsel includes the right to communicate and consult freely with his attorney in private, both prior to and during the trial, and at reasonable hours and intervals.

a. *Incompetent counsel*—The general rule is that where the accused has employed an attorney of his *own choice* he may **not** appeal a conviction on the basis of such attorney's inexperience, lack of skill, lack of preparation, improper advice, or errors of judgment. An attorney is deemed incompetent only if his advice and representation is so lacking in diligence and competence that the rights and protections guaranteed by due process are denied the accused (e.g., a fair trial). If the attorney's lack of competence deprived the accused of a fair trial, the conviction will be declared void on the grounds that he was denied his Constitutional right to the assistance of counsel.

2. *At Every Stage of Prosecution*—The right to the assistance of counsel applies to *all* felony prosecutions and to *any* misdemeanor prosecutions which carry a penalty of **incarceration** (jail or imprisonment). In other words, it is unconstitutional to jail or imprison a person for conviction of **any** crime unless such person was given an opportunity to be represented by counsel at his trial. (**Note:** Any conviction obtained in violation of the right to counsel is *invalid*.)

The general rule is that the right to counsel extends to every "critical pretrial stage" of the prosecution. Any *"confrontation"* of an accused person and an identifying witness at any *out-of-court* identification proceeding is considered a "critical stage" of the criminal prosecution. The Supreme Court has held that an accused is entitled to be assisted by counsel (1) prior to any questioning when *in custody* (or otherwise deprived of his freedom by the authorities), (2) during the *preliminary hearing*, (3) during his *arraignment* and acceptance of a plea, (4) at his *trial*, and (5) at *sentencing*.

Under *Miranda* the right to counsel has also been held to apply *before* questioning to any "custodial interrogation" of a **suspect** by law enforcement officers. For example, a *suspect* (not an accused) who is required to give a demonstration of his voice in order to possibly identify him as the perpetrator of a crime is entitled to the assistance of counsel before doing so; a failure to warn a suspect of his right to counsel is a violation of the 6th and 14th Amendments.

a. *Police lineup (right to counsel)*—Both an accused *and* a suspect have a Constitutional right to counsel at a police identification (out-of-court) *lineup*. If an accused was denied his right to counsel at a police lineup at which he was *identified*, testimony as to the lineup identification of the accused is *inadmissible* at the trial. [**Note:** An in-court identification of the accused by the identifying witness at the lineup is inadmissible unless the identification is "independent" of the lineup (e.g., eye-witness observation at the time of the crime).]

b. *Photographic displays (no right to counsel)*—The Supreme Court has held that a person does *not* have a right to counsel at a pretrial photographic display where a witness attempts to identify the perpetrator of a crime, even if the photographic display is conducted *after* an indictment. In other words, neither a person accused of crime nor a suspect has a right to counsel at an out-of-court pretrial identification where a witness is being shown a photographic display and asked to identify the person who committed the crime (e.g., "mug shots").

3. *Indigents Have Right To Counsel*—In 1963 (*Gideon v. Wainwright*) the Supreme Court ruled that when a person accused with committing a felony is *financially unable* to employ an attorney, the court **must** appoint one to represent him (*unless* the accused has competently and intelli-

gently waived his right to counsel). The Supreme Court has since ruled that, in the absence of a knowing and intelligent waiver, an accused has the right to an attorney in **any** criminal action which carries a punishment of *jail* or *imprisonment*, whether classified as petty, misdemeanor, or felony, and where the accused cannot afford an attorney, the state **must** provide one to represent him. [*Argersinger v. Hamlin (1972)*] In other words, in the absence of a valid waiver no person may be jailed or imprisoned for any crime unless he was represented by counsel at his trial.

The test to determine whether an accused is an indigent is whether he is **able** to employ counsel, not whether he "ought to be able" to employ counsel. Due process requires that a reasonable opportunity for the preparation of the accused's defense must be allowed between the time counsel is appointed and the date of trial. (**Note:** Although an indigent is entitled to free counsel, he is *not* entitled to select a particular attorney as his court appointed counsel.) Statutes in a **majority** of states provide for the appoint of a *public defender* to represent indigents accused of crime. The public defender becomes attorney for the accused for all purposes of the case to the same extent as if the accused had personally employed him.

§10. WAIVER OF CONSTITUTIONAL PROTECTIONS (PERSONAL RIGHTS ONLY)

A. CANNOT WAIVE RIGHTS WHERE STATE HAS INTEREST (PUBLIC POLICY)

1. *Due Process and Equal Protection (5th and 14th Amendments)*—The term "waiver" is generally defined as an intentional and voluntary relinquishment or abandonment of a **known** right or privilege. There is a rebuttable presumption against the waiver of fundamental Constitutional rights. However, the general rule is that an accused may waive any Constitutional privilege or right which is **personal** to himself, *provided* such waiver is not against "public policy" (e.g., when the state *also* has an interest). For example, the right to a fair and impartial

trial (due process) *cannot* be waived. Provided it is not against public policy, the accused may waive any known Constitutional right by express consent, by failure to assert the right in time, or by conduct which is inconsistent with an intent to waive. (**Note:** Where the accused does not know his Constitutional rights, he *cannot* waive them.)

2. *Unreasonable Search and Seizure (4th Amendment)* — The Constitutional right to be secure against unreasonable searches and seizures may be waived by *consenting* to a warrantless search and seizure. A search made pursuant to a valid consent may be made without a warrant and without probable cause. However, the person consenting must have had the authority to consent and the consent must be voluntary and not coerced. There can be **no** consent where there is a warrant, even if the warrant later turns out to be invalid.

The lawful owner or occupier of premises may consent to its search. Similarly, any joint owner may consent to a search of premises and items over which he has control, provided the suspect is *absent*. If the suspect is present and objects to the search, the joint owner *cannot* give a valid consent. Similarly, the lawful owner, possessor, or custodian of property (not premises) may consent to its search or seizure, even if such property contains evidence which will incriminate another person.

A consent search is reasonable only if it does not exceed the actual consent given. For example, if government agents obtain consent to search for a stolen item, they must limit their activity to that which is necessary to search for such an item and may not rummage through private documents and personal papers. However, under the "plain view" rule, when police officers are on the premises pursuant to a valid *consent* to a search, any item falling into their plain view may properly be seized, even if the item is not connected with their purpose in entering.

3. *Right To Be Present (5th Amendment)* — The right to be present at all stages of the trial is not absolute. In the **majority** of states the accused can *waive* his right to be

personally present at every stage of the trial. The rationale is that the right to be present is essentially for the benefit of the accused and since the accused may waive his trial by pleading guilty, he may also waive his right to be present.

The accused **cannot** waive his right to be present when (1) he is in *custody* or (2) he is charged with a *capital* crime (death penalty). An accused who is in custody cannot waive his right to be present because his presence or absence is at the will of the state rather than at his own will. An accused charged with a capital crime cannot waive his right to be present because the severity of the punishment requires his presence. However, if an accused *escapes* from custody and flees, he will be deemed to have waived his right and the trial may be completed without him. [(**Note:** An accused who is free on bail may waive his right to be present at the trial merely by his *voluntary failure to appear* at trial (voluntary absence).]

4. *Privilege Against Self-Incrimination (5th Amendment)* — The Constitutional prohibition against compelled self-incrimination may be waived at any stage of the proceedings. The waiver must be based upon knowledge and intelligent choice; that is, the privilege must be *knowingly* and *voluntarily* waived. For example, an accused may waive his privilege against self-incrimination by testifying in his own behalf. (**Note:** Although an accused may have waived the privilege, he may *not* be compelled to perform an act or experiment which might aid in connecting him with the crime and establish his guilt.)

5. *Right To Speedy Trial (6th Amendment)* — The Constitutional right to speedy trial may be waived. The accused waives his right to a speedy trial when he requests a continuance or postponement of his trial or where he agrees to a delay sought by the prosecution. Similarly, a voluntary plea of guilty waives any delays which may have occurred up to that time.

6. *Right To Public Trial (6th Amendment)* — The right to public trial is a personal right and may be waived by the accused.

7. *Right To Jury (6th Amendment)* — The right to a jury trial is a personal right which the accused may waive, provided he does so knowingly and with full understanding of the consequences of such waiver.

8. *Right To Confrontation (6th Amendment)* — The right of an accused to be confronted by witnesses against him is a personal right which may be waived by the accused.

9. *Right To Counsel (6th Amendment)* — The Constitutional right to the assistance of counsel is a personal right which may be waived by the accused. However, the general rule is that a waiver may not be accepted until the judge has determined that the accused fully understands the nature of the charge, the element of the crime, the pleas and defenses available, and the punishment that may be imposed.

The trial court is justified in imposing an attorney on an accused against his will if, in the judge's discretion, it appears that the accused is mentally incompetent or not sui juris (e.g., capable of assuming legal responsibility) at the time of the trial. If the accused is sui juris and mentally competent, he may waive counsel, rely on his own skill, and conduct his defense in person without the assistance of counsel, provided he does so with full knowledge and understanding of the risks involved.

II. *AFTER CONVICTION*

§1. RIGHTS REGARDING SENTENCING (PROCEDURAL)

A. LEGAL CONSEQUENCES OF GUILT

1. *Judicial Act Declaring Punishment* — A "sentence" (or judgment) is the judicial act of a court which formally declares the legal consequences of the accused's guilt. In other words, it is the punishment or penalty imposed by the court upon an accused who has been found guilty. The term "conviction" means either a finding of guilt by a plea of guilty or nolo contendere, a verdict or judgment of guilty, or sentencing on such pleas, verdict, or judgment. It applies only to **criminal** proceedings and *not* to civil or administrative proceedings. The general rule is that the forfeiture of bail (failure to appear in court for trial) is also equivalent to a conviction.

   The U.S. Supreme Court has held that sentencing is a *critical stage* of a criminal prosecution at which an accused has a constitutional right to the *assistance of counsel*. The absence of counsel during sentencing is a denial of due process. Similarly, the accused has the right to be *present* at the time the sentence is pronounced. Under the common law, when even the slightest imprisonment or other corporal (physical) punishment is to be inflicted, the accused *must* be present in court when the sentence is pronounced. (**Note:** The right to be present at sentencing is separate and apart from the right to be present at the trial.)

   a. *Allocution* — The term "allocution" is the statutory right which a person convicted of a felony has, before imposition of the sentence, to make a statement to the court as to why sentence should not be pronounced against him. Federal statutes and most state statutes require that *before* sentence is imposed, the trial court must give the convicted defendant an opportunity to speak in his own behalf as to why he should not be sentenced or why his punishment should be lessened.

2. *Must Be Definite And Certain* — A sentence must be definite, certain, and not dependent on any contingency or condition. The sentence must conform strictly to the applicable statute, and any variation from its provisions, either in the nature or the degree of punishment imposed, renders the judgment **void** (e.g., a sentence of imprisonment cannot be imposed where a statute provides only for punishment by a fine).

In the **majority** of jurisdictions the beginning date of a sentence of imprisonment runs from the date when the convicted defendent is *received* at either the prison or jail to commence service of the sentence, or at a place of detention to await transportation to such prison or jail. Unless otherwise provided by statute, a sentence that does not specify a beginning date is presumed to run from the day it was imposed. If a prisoner escapes or is released on bail, such time out of prison is *not* considered part of the sentence to be served. In other words, if any part of the sentence lapses without imprisonment, the sentence is still valid; it is merely *unexecuted*. (**Note:** Where a defendant is re-convicted at a retrial following a successful appeal, the new sentence cannot be greater than the previous sentence. Also, credit must be given for any time served under the original sentence.)

a. *Concurrent or consecutive (cumulative) sentences* — "Concurrent" sentences are sentences which operate *simultaneously*; that is, each sentence is to commence at the same time. "Consecutive" (or "cumulative") sentences are sentences which immediately *follow* each other in a regular order, with no interval or break; that is, the time under the second sentence is to commence when the first ends, and so on through the last sentence.

b. ***Excessive or inadequate sentence*** — When a sentence is in *excess* of what the law permits, the legal and authorized portion of the sentence is not void. A defendant under an excessive sentence must serve the *legal portion* of the sentence before he can be discharged. Similarly, a sentence of *less* than the minimum punishment permitted by law is not void. It is subject to correction, but it is not a ground for
  • reversing the conviction.

When there is a verdict of guilty on each of *two or more indictments* consolidated for trial, or under a single indictment charging two or more distinct crimes, the general rule is that the court may impose a sentence on each separate indictment or on each separate count that is supported by the evidence. However, in order for separate crimes charged in one indictment to carry separate punishments, they must rest on distinct criminal acts. That is, each crime requires proof of some fact or element not required to establish the other crime. The sentence imposed should not be for the total time in gross, but for a specified time under **each** indictment or count. The general rule is that if the court fails to specify otherwise, the term of imprisonment on the second or subsequent sentence runs *concurrently* with the first.

B. PROBATION

1. *Suspending Sentence Before Commitment* — Probation is the *suspending* of a sentence for a specific or reasonable length of time **prior** to commitment. There is a split of authority as to whether a court, in the absence of statute, has the power to "suspend" sentence. Some states follow the early common law rule that a court has inherent power to suspend a sentence in whole or in part. However, most states provide that a court cannot suspend a sentence unless the power to do so is authorized by *statute*. (**Note:** Federal statutes grant the power to suspend sentence in *federal* criminal prosecutions and to place the defendant on probation for such period and upon such terms and conditions as the court deems best.)

a. *No probation permitted after sentence begins* — A trial court *cannot* set aside a valid sentence *after* it has been put into execution; that is, the power to grant probation cannot be exercised after a sentence is begun. (**Note:** The sentence may only be set aside by an *appellate* court.) In other words, after *commitment* of the defendant, the trial court cannot impose a different sentence which either increases, decreases, or otherwise modifies the punishment. A sentence that attempts to do so is **void** and the original sentence remains in force.

2. *Revocation of Probation*—Upon violation of the conditions of probation (e.g., a subsequent criminal conviction and sentence occurring during probation), the court may revoke the probation. A violation of the conditions of probation is *not* a crime in itself. Thus, a proceeding to revoke probation is not a criminal prosecution, and a formal trial is not required (unless required by statute). If probation was granted by suspending the "imposition" of a sentence, the order revoking probation requires that the original sentence be *imposed*. If probation was granted by suspending the "execution" of a sentence, the order revoking probation requires that the original sentence imposed now be *executed*.

A convicted defendant, released on probation, is entitled to *notice* and a *hearing* on the issue of whether he has broken the conditions of probation before such probation may be revoked. The defendant has a right to be represented by *counsel* only if, on the facts of the case, such representation is necessary to a fair hearing. If revocation of probation involves the imposition of a *new* sentence, the defendant has a right to be represented by counsel and must be informed that he has such right.

§2. RIGHTS REGARDING PUNISHMENT (SUBSTANTIVE)

A. EXECUTION OF SENTENCE IS PUNISHMENT

1. *Can Only Impose Punishment Prescribed By Statute*— The term "punishment" is generally defined as the infliction, by authority of law, of penalty, suffering, or confinement of a person under the sentence of a court for some

crime committed by him. The sentence of the court is the **authority** to punish a convicted defendant. A convicted defendant does *not* commence his punishment at the time a sentence is pronounced by the court. The punishment commences when the defendant is delivered into the custody of government officers to be committed to imprisonment under the sentence.

The power to determine the punishment to be imposed for commission of a crime rests with the legislature, **not** with the courts. The power of a legislature to prescribe punishment for a crime is subject only to constitutional prohibitions regarding excessive fines, cruel and unusual punishments, and the due process and equal protection clauses of the 14th Amendment. For example, punishments based on arbitrary or unreasonable classifications, such as race or color, are invalid. (**Note:** The guarantee of equal protection of the laws does *not* affect the right of a state to punish one crime more severely than another.)

In all states the punishments to be imposed are determined by the legislature. The punishment to be inflicted must conform to the law at the time of the *sentence*. Also, the extent of the punishment imposed for conviction of a crime must fit the nature and seriousness of the crime (e.g., twenty years hard labor for falsifying a public record is a cruel and unusual punishment which violates the 8th Amendment). In a **majority** of states the punishment is assessed by the *judge*, not by the jury. In a **minority** of states the *jury* is authorized to either assess the punishment to be imposed or to recommend alternative punishments.

B. PUNISHMENTS PERMITTED

1. *Imprisonment* —In the absence of Constitutional prohibition, the legislature may prescribe imprisonment (confinement) as punishment for a crime. The imprisonment may be for a term of years (definite sentence) or for the lifetime of the defendant (indeterminate sentence). Under a **definite sentence** the defendant is sentenced to serve a *specific* number of years in prison. The general rule is that the defendant is eligible for conditional work release or parole after serving one-third of his sentence.

Under an **indeterminate sentence** the defendant is sentenced to be confined for an *indefinite* number of years (e.g., "no more than" a specified number of years) or to a minimum and maximum number of years. If the defendant is sentenced to an indefinite number of years he is eligible for parole when prison authorities believe he is "rehabilitated". If the defendant is sentenced to a minimum and maximum number of years he is eligible for parole once the minimum is served. (**Note:** An indeterminate sentence may also consist of committing the defendant to a special institution or hospital to receive treatment for drug addiction, alcoholism, or mental illness until rehabilitated.)

2. *Death Penalty* —The imposition of the death penalty does **not** per se violate the 8th Amendment prohibition against cruel and unusual punishment. In other words, the legislature is not constitutionally prohibited from prescribing the death penalty for certain serious crimes. In those jurisdictions which permit the death penalty it is *not* cruel and unusual punishment to execute the death sentence by shooting, hanging, electrocuting, or lethally gassing the condemned person. However, the U.S. Supreme Court has held that a death penalty **is** unconstitutional if it (1) is to be inflicted in a *painful or inhumane* manner or (2) is imposed in an arbitrary or manner. (**Note:** The place where an execution is to be carried out must be within the boundaries of the state having jurisdiction of the crime.)

3. *Fines* —In the absence of Constitutional prohibition, the legislature may prescribe a *fine* as punishment for a crime. A "fine" is a pecuniary (monetary) punishment, the amount of which may be fixed by the legislature or left to the discretion of the court. Committing the defendant to jail until a fine is paid is *not* considered part of the punishment. The punishment is the fine; the imprisonment is the method of enforcing payment of the fine (e.g., executing the sentence). In other words, confinement of the defendant in order to satisfy an unpaid fine is **not** an unconstitutional imprisonment for *debt*.

Statutes in many states permit confinement of a defendant for *failure* to pay the assessed fine. However, the defendant must be given a reasonable time to make such payment. Imprisonment for failure to make *immediate* payment of a fine violates the equal protection clause of the 14th Amendment.

Payment of a fine may be *enforced* by imprisonment, but *only* when such enforcement is prescribed by the court when it imposes the sentence. However, such imprisonment cannot *exceed* the maximum statutory time of imprisonment prescribed by the legislature for the particular crime. If the confinement is beyond the statutory maximum term, it is a denial of equal protection under the 14th Amendment.

C. PUNISHMENTS NOT PERMITTED

1. *Banishment*—A sentence which banishes a person convicted of crime from the jurisdiction of the court is impliedly prohibited by public policy. Although such a sentence is not considered cruel and unusual punishment, it is generally held to be *void*. Similarly, the suspension (or reduction) of a sentence based on the condition that the convicted person leave the state or county, is *void*. [**Note:** A sentence of banishment may be imposed by a *federal* court on foreign citizens who commit crimes in the United States (e.g., deportation).]

2. *Cruel and Unusual (8th and 14th Amendment)*—The 8th Amendment to the U.S. Constitution *prohibits* the infliction of cruel and unusual punishments. The 8th Amendment has been incorporated into the 14th Amendment and now applies to all state actions. The Constitutional prohibition against cruel and unusual punishments is intended as a *limitation* on legislative bodies when prescribing punishment. For example, a penalty that is greater than any previously prescribed, known, or inflicted is considered cruel and unusual.

In federal criminal prosecutions, imprisonment in "solitary confinement" does *not* violate either the 8th or 14th Amendment prohibition against cruel and unusual punishment. However, solitary confinement may violate a *state* constitutional provision. Similarly, punishment by imprisonment at "hard labor" is *not*, of itself, considered cruel and unusual. However, hard labor may be a cruel and unusual punishment if it is *substantially greater* than that warranted by the crime committed. For example, six years imprisonment at hard labor for picking flowers in a public park is a cruel and unusual punishment.

a. **Death penalty**—A state may impose the death penalty provided the execution thereof is not inflicted in a **painful and inhumane manner.** A statute which permits the execution of the death penalty in a painful and inhumane manner violates the 8th Amendment prohibition against cruel and unusual punishments. For example, a statute which permits execution of a death sentence by poisoning is unconstitutional. (**Note:** Although Constitutionally permitted, statutes in many states prohibit the imposition of the death penalty. What were formerly capital crimes in these states are now punished by life imprisonment.)

The U.S. Supreme Court has recently held that the **discretionary** imposition of the death penalty also constitutes cruel and unusual punishment. [*Furman v. Georgia (1972)*] The court held that a statute which permits the jury to impose or withhold the death penalty as it sees fit, without any governing standards, constitutes cruel and unusual punishment. In other words, a statutory death penalty is per se cruel and unusual punishment (and therefore unconstitutional) if the *procedure* by which the death penalty is imposed is discretionary (e.g., if it permits arbitrary imposition of the death penalty).

Under the *Furman* decision, the imposition and carrying out of the death penalty constitutes cruel and unusual punishment when a *jury*, under state law, has *discretion* to determine whether or not to impose the death penalty. For example, a statute which requires imposition of a mandatory death sentence, but does not allow a jury to consider evidence of mitigating circumstances or the personal characteristics of the accused, and affords no specific detailed guidelines as to the relevance of such evidence in the determination of whether a death sentence is appropriate, violates the 8th and 14th Amendment and is invalid.

3. LOSS OF RIGHTS "DURING" PUNISHMENT (PROCEDURAL)

A. SUSPENSION OF CIVIL RIGHTS

1. *Imprisonment for Term Less Than Life (Majority)*—In the **majority** of states a person sentenced for a term *less than life* forfeits all public offices and private trusts; however, his civil rights are only *suspended* during the term of his sentence. In other words, the defendant does **not** lose citizenship, but merely some of his rights and privileges as a citizen, most of which are automatically restored when the sentence has been completed. (**Note:** In the **majority** of states, ex-felons are *not* allowed to vote, to hold public office, or to serve on juries. A few states provide that if an ex-felon is not convicted again within a certain number of years, his right to vote will be returned.)

   The suspension of civil rights begins when the defendant is actually imprisoned under the imposed sentence, *not* at the time the sentence is rendered. A prisoner has certain Constitutional rights even while imprisoned. In a **majority** of jurisdictions a prisoner may be sued while imprisoned, may file suit while imprisoned, and may also take, hold, and dispose of both real and personal property. A prisoner also has the right to communicate with his lawyer, to receive and send out "uncensored" mail to and from his attorney, to prepare and file his own case, and to have access to a court.

2. *Statutory "Civil Death" (Minority)*—Under the early common law, a person's civil rights were extinguished upon conviction of a **felony**. The extinguishment of such rights was termed "civil death". In a **minority** of states, a modified form of civil death is provided by statute. For example, under statutory civil death the convict's property may be subjected to the payment of his debts by foreclosure; however, it does *not* include divesting the

convict of his estate by an outright sale. (**Note:** Statutory civil death does *not* apply to persons under death sentences.)

B. PAROLE

1. *After Serving Portion of Sentence*—The term "parole" means a *conditional release* of a convict before he has served his entire sentence; that is, the remaining portion of the convict's sentence is **suspended**. The convict released on parole is called a "parolee". If a convict has been given a definite sentence (e.g., three years imprisonment) the general rule is that he will be elegible for parole after serving *one-third* of his total sentence (e.g., after one year) or until he has become rehabilitated. If a convict has been indeterminately sentenced to a minimum and a maximum period of time (e.g., two to eight years) the general rule is that he will be eligible for a parole after he has completed his *minimum* sentence (e.g., after two years).

   If the parolee fulfills the conditions of his release, he will be granted an absolute *discharge* from the balance of his sentence. If the parolee violates any condition of his parole, a warrant can be issued for his arrest and return to prison. Most states impose the following conditions as part of the parole: the parolee must report periodically to a parole officer; may not leave a certain geographical area; may not consume any alcohol or drugs; may not associate with persons having bad reputations or criminal records; may not possess a deadly weapon or firearm; and may not marry without consulting and obtaining permission from his parole officer.

   a. *The parole board*—The determination of whether or not a prisoner will be released early is usually made by a parole board which holds a hearing and decides one of the following: (1) to grant parole effective immediately; (2) to grant parole conditionally; (3) to grant parole which takes effect sometime in the future (e.g., after a work release program or a half-way house); or, (4) deny parole (usually on the basis of recommendations made by prison officials).

b. ***Revocation of parole***—In order to revoke a parole, the parole board must hold a parole revocation *hearing*. Due process requires that a parolee be afforded (1) an informal "preliminary" hearing before a neutral hearing *officer* not involved in the case who determines if there is probable cause to believe the parolee violated his parole; and, (2) a "revocation" hearing before a neutral hearing *body*, with written notice of the charge. At the revocation hearing a parolee has a right to be represented by counsel, to appear at the hearing, to testify, to present evidence and witnesses, and to confront his accusers.

c. ***Pardon, commutation, amnesty, and reprieve distinguished***—A **parole** releases a convicted prisoner *before* the expiration of his sentence, subject to certain conditions. It is similar to a pardon in that it suspends the further execution of a punishment already being inflicted. A **pardon** releases a convicted prisoner from the *entire* punishment imposed and from all disabilities as a consequence of the conviction. It terminates punishment and blots out the existence of guilt as though the defendant had never committed the crime.

A **commutation** is a *substitution* of a lesser penalty for the one originally imposed. **Amnesty** is the *abolition* and forgetfulness of the crime and is applied only to crimes against the "sovereignty" of the state. A **reprieve** merely *postpones* the execution of a sentence for a period of time; it does *not* defeat the sentence (e.g., where the prisoner has become insane or is a female prisoner and has become pregnant).

INDEX
Criminal Procedure